MILITARY TACTICS FOR HOME DEFENSE

From Survivor to Strategist, Defend Your Loved Ones by Making Your Home a Secure Survival Fortress

Tim Enry

© 2024 Military Tactics For Home Defense All rights reserved. This document is for informational use related to 'Military Bug-In.' The publisher accepts no liability for any harm from applying or misapplying its contents. Unauthorized copying, sharing, or sending of this book, in full or partially, is forbidden. Trademarks and brand names cited are owned by their respective holders. This book is offered 'as is,' with no expressed or implied guarantees.

CONTENTS

Introduction 6

Why Bugging In Matters 6

Overview of the Guide 7

Chapter 1: Understanding Bugging In 9

The Concept of Bugging In 9

Definition and Origins of Bugging In 9

The Psychology Behind Staying Put 10

When and Why to Choose Bugging In 11

Assessing Bug-In vs. Bug-Out 11

Environmental and Geographical Factors 12

Preparing Your Home for Bugging In 14

Initial Home Assessment 14

Creating a Bug-In Plan 15

Common Mistakes and Avoidance Strategies 17

Overconfidence and Complacency 17

Effective Communication Strategies 18

Chapter 2: Mental and Physical Preparedness 20

Developing the Military Mindset 20

Understanding the Military Mentality 20

Cultivating Mental Toughness 21

Building Physical Resilience 22

Assessing Physical Fitness for Survival 22

Developing a Survival Fitness Routine 24

Stress Management and Psychological Fortitude 25

Recognizing and Managing Stress 25

Building Psychological Fortitude 26

Maintaining Morale and Motivation 28

Chapter 3: Home Security and Fortification 30

Assessing and Strengthening Home Security 30

Conducting a Home Security Audit 30

Enhancing Entry Point Security 31

Implementing Home Surveillance Systems 32

Building an Impenetrable Fortress 33

Fortifying the Perimeter 33

Reinforcing Walls and Structural Elements 35

Installing Defensive Systems 38

Creating Safe and Panic Rooms 41

Designing a Safe Room 41

Constructing a Panic Room 42

Stocking Your Safe/Panic Room 44

Chapter 4: Long-Term Food Storage 46

Principles of Food Stockpiling 46

Assessing Family Nutritional Needs 46

Calculating Food Storage Needs 47

Selecting Storage Containers and Methods 48

Best Foods for Long-Term Storage 49

Staple Foods for Energy and Balance 49

Nutrient-Dense Foods for Health 51

Long-Lasting Packaged Foods 52

Rotating and Maintaining Food Reserve 53

Establishing a Food Rotation System 53

Monitoring Food Quality and Shelf Life 54

Using Stockpiled Food in Daily Meals 55

Audio Version 58

Chapter 5: Water Security and Purification 59

Securing a Reliable Water Supply 59

Assessing Household Water Needs 59

Identifying Local Water Sources 60

Rainwater Harvesting System Setup 61

Storage Solutions for Long-Term Use 62

Choosing Water Storage Containers 62

Short vs. Long-Term Water Storage 64

Preventing Water Contamination 65

Purification Techniques for Safe Water 66

Understanding Water Contaminants 66

Boiling and Filtration Methods 67

Advanced Water Purification Systems 68

Building a DIY Water Purification System 69

Chapter 6: Off-Grid Energy Solutions 72

Powering Your Home Off-Grid 72

Assessing Your Energy Needs 72

Designing an Off-Grid Energy System 74

Backup Power Sources 75

Exploring Solar, Wind, Generator Options 76

Solar Power Systems 76

Wind Power for Home Defense 78

Generator Backup Power and Safety 79

Energy Conservation Strategies 80

Reducing Energy Consumption at Home 80

Seasonal Energy Conservation Tips 82

Smart Energy Management Systems 83

Chapter 7: Medical Preparedness 85

Building a Home First Aid Kit 85

Basic First Aid Kit Components 85

Advanced Medical Supplies 86

Customizing First Aid Kits 87

Essential Medications and Uses 88

Over-the-Counter Medications 88

Managing Prescription Medications 90

Natural Remedies and Supplements 91

Managing Health Conditions Independently 92

Recognizing and Treating Common Ailments 93

Long-Term Management of Chronic Conditions 95

Emergency Medical Procedures 96

Psychological First Aid in Crises 97

Chapter 8: Crisis Communication and Networking 99

Emergency Communication Systems 99

Communication Needs in a Crisis 99

Choosing Emergency Communication Devices 100

Communication Equipment Maintenance 101

Backup Communication Strategies 103

Chapter 9: Essential Survival Gear 105

Navy SEAL Gear for Home Defense 105

Firearms for Home Defense 105

Non-Lethal Defense Options 106

Home Security Systems 107

Tactical Gear for Home Security 109

Must-Have Tools for Crisis Scenarios 110

Essential Cutting Tools for Emergencies 110

Fire-Starting Tools 111

Water Filtration and Purification Tools 112

Essential Shelter and Sleeping Gear 114

Emergency Communication Tools 115

Stockpiling and Storing Survival Gear 116

Organizing Your Gear 116

Gear Storage Best Practices 117

Long-Term Storage Considerations 118

Assembling Emergency Kits 120

Chapter 10: Tactical Self-Defense Strategies 122

Basic Self-Defense Techniques 122

    Awareness and Situational Preparedness 122

    Physical Defense Techniques 123

    De-escalation and Conflict Resolution 124

Tactical Tools and Weapons 125

    Tactical Weapons for Home Defense 125

    Tactical Tools Training and Proficiency 127

    Legal Aspects of Home Defense Weapons 128

Defensive Tactics Against Intruders 129

    Establishing a Defensive Perimeter 129

    Safe Room Tactics and Protocols 130

    Responding to a Home Invasion 132

Conclusion 134

    Key Concepts and Strategies Recap 134

    Final Thoughts on Preparedness and Resilience 135

    Next Steps in Preparedness 135

Introduction

Why Bugging In Matters

In the realm of military strategy, the concept of holding ground and fortifying one's position has been a cornerstone of defense for centuries. This principle is not only applicable on the battlefield but also translates seamlessly into civilian emergency preparedness, particularly in the context of bugging in. Bugging in—choosing to stay and secure your home rather than evacuate in the face of danger—embodies a strategic approach rooted in military wisdom. It leverages the advantage of familiar terrain, the ability to stockpile and manage resources efficiently, and the psychological benefit of defending a known stronghold.

The military approach to bugging in emphasizes detailed planning, starting with a comprehensive assessment of your home's current security posture. This involves identifying potential vulnerabilities in physical structures such as doors, windows, and walls. Recommendations for materials and fortification techniques are specific: for instance, doors should be reinforced with steel security doors that have deadbolt locks, while windows can be secured with impact-resistant film and bars to prevent easy entry. Walls, often overlooked, can be fortified with materials like sandbags for temporary protection or by using construction techniques that incorporate reinforced concrete for long-term resilience.

Resource management is another critical aspect borrowed from military strategy. This includes calculating water and food supplies based on the number of occupants and the duration of potential isolation. For water, the recommendation is to store at least one gallon per person per day, with a diverse storage solution encompassing large barrels for long-term storage and smaller, portable containers for immediate use. Food stockpiling strategies are equally detailed, focusing on a balanced mix of macronutrients and vitamins, shelf-stable items like canned goods, dry grains, and legumes, and methods of preservation such as freezing and dehydration that can extend the shelf life of perishables.

Surveillance and intelligence gathering are also integral to the military approach to bugging in, adapted for civilian use through the installation of security cameras, motion detectors, and alarm systems. These systems should offer remote access capabilities, allowing homeowners to monitor their property even when not physically present. The choice of equipment is specific, with recommendations for cameras that offer night vision, weather resistance, and wide-angle lenses for comprehensive coverage of the property's perimeter.

Training and preparedness form the backbone of effective bugging in, mirroring the military's emphasis on drills and readiness. This includes regular family emergency drills that cover scenarios like home invasions, fires, and medical emergencies, ensuring that every family member knows their role and actions to take under stress. Additionally, physical fitness is highlighted as a critical component of preparedness, with a focus on developing strength, endurance, and agility through routines that incorporate bodyweight exercises, cardiovascular training, and flexibility work.

In essence, the military-endorsed strategy of bugging in is a multifaceted approach that prioritizes security, resource management, intelligence, and preparedness. By adopting these principles, individuals can transform their homes into secure fortresses, ready to withstand a range of emergencies. This approach not only enhances physical safety but also provides peace of mind, knowing that one is well-prepared to protect and sustain their loved ones in times of crisis.

Overview of the Guide

This guide is meticulously crafted to equip you with the knowledge and skills necessary to transform your home into a fortress of survival, drawing upon military strategies and principles tailored for civilian application. You will embark on a comprehensive journey through the intricacies of bugging in, starting with a deep dive into the concept itself, understanding its origins, and the psychological shift required to adopt this survival strategy effectively. The guide emphasizes the importance of assessing your situation, taking into account environmental and geographical factors that influence the decision to bug in, thereby ensuring that your choice is informed and strategic.

Preparing your home for bugging in is dissected into actionable steps, beginning with an initial home assessment to identify vulnerabilities, followed by the creation of a customized bug-in plan that involves all family members, fostering a unified approach to home defense. Common pitfalls in preparation are highlighted, with guidance on how to avoid them, ensuring that overconfidence and communication failures do not undermine your efforts.

Physical and mental preparedness are addressed in detail, presenting methods to develop a military mindset that includes understanding military principles, cultivating mental toughness, and building physical resilience. Techniques for managing stress and building psychological fortitude are shared, recognizing the importance of maintaining morale and motivation in prolonged crises.

The guide delves into home security and fortification, offering a step-by-step approach to assessing and strengthening home security, enhancing entry point security, and implementing surveillance and monitoring systems. Building an impenetrable fortress involves fortifying the perimeter, reinforcing walls and structural elements, and installing defensive systems, with special attention given to creating safe rooms and panic rooms.

Long-term food storage, water security and purification, off-grid energy solutions, medical preparedness, crisis communication, essential survival gear, and tactical self-defense strategies are comprehensively covered. Each section provides specific recommendations for materials, tools, and techniques, ensuring that you are well-equipped to defend your loved ones and maintain a secure, self-sufficient living environment in the face of any crisis.

Chapter 1: Understanding Bugging In

The Concept of Bugging In

Definition and Origins of Bugging In

Bugging in, a term now synonymous with the strategic choice to remain in one's home during emergencies or crises, finds its roots deeply embedded in military doctrine and the instinctual human drive for safety and security. This concept, while seemingly straightforward, encompasses a rich history and a complex array of considerations that have evolved over time. The origins of bugging in can be traced back to ancient times when fortresses and castles were the ultimate safe havens against invaders. In these historical contexts, the idea was to utilize the home or stronghold not just as a place of refuge but as a base of operations, a place where one could sustain oneself while under siege. The modern interpretation of bugging in, while less about repelling medieval invaders, still carries the core principle of using one's residence as a fortified shelter, leveraging it as a strategic advantage in the face of modern threats such as natural disasters, pandemics, or civil unrest.

The military influence on the concept of bugging in is unmistakable, with principles of fortification, logistics, and psychological warfare all playing roles in how individuals and families prepare their homes for potential crises. From the perspective of military strategy, bugging in is akin to holding the high ground, a position of strength that offers significant advantages over being exposed or on the move. This strategy involves detailed planning around the fortification of physical structures, the stockpiling of resources such as food and water, and the establishment of communication and surveillance systems to maintain awareness of the surrounding environment. The psychological aspect of bugging in, deeply rooted in the human psyche's need for a safe and secure environment, is also a critical element of this strategy. The familiarity and emotional attachment to one's home provide a morale boost and a sense of purpose in defending and maintaining it, which can be crucial in long-term survival scenarios.

In the context of emergency preparedness, bugging in is defined as the decision to stay put and fortify one's home instead of evacuating in the face of potential danger. This decision is not made lightly and involves a comprehensive assessment of various factors, including the nature of the threat, the likelihood of its impact on the immediate area, and the readiness of the home to serve as a safe and sustainable shelter. The strategic choice to bug in is predicated on the understanding that in many scenarios, the home can be transformed into a secure fortress, equipped with necessary supplies, defenses, and survival mechanisms to weather the storm, whatever it may be. This transformation requires meticulous planning, from reinforcing doors and windows to ensuring a reliable supply of water and food, all aimed at creating a self-sufficient sanctuary that can support its inhabitants for an extended period.

The evolution of bugging in as a survival strategy reflects a broader understanding of the complexities and challenges of modern emergencies. It underscores a pragmatic and disciplined approach to preparedness, emphasizing resilience, adaptability, and the strategic use of available resources. For those who adopt this strategy, bugging in is more than just a tactical decision; it is a comprehensive lifestyle choice that prioritizes the safety and security of one's family and home. It is a testament to the enduring human spirit's ability to prepare for, adapt to, and overcome the myriad challenges posed by an ever-changing world.

The Psychology Behind Staying Put

The mental preparation required for bugging in is a critical component of your survival strategy, demanding a significant shift in mindset from the more instinctive reaction to flee—bugging out—to the strategic choice of staying put. This decision is not merely a physical act of remaining within the confines of your home but a profound psychological commitment to withstand and endure the challenges of isolation and potential long-term confinement. The transition from a mindset of mobility and escape to one of fortification and resilience involves several key psychological adjustments.

Firstly, embracing the concept of bugging in necessitates an acceptance of your home not just as a living space but as a survival sanctuary. This means viewing every room, every resource, and every aspect of your home's layout with a strategic eye. It involves a mental mapping of your space in terms of its defensive capabilities, its potential to sustain life over extended periods, and its capacity to provide psychological comfort and stability. The familiarity of your home becomes a double-edged sword; while it offers comfort and a sense of security, it also requires you to reevaluate and sometimes repurpose these familiar spaces for survival.

Secondly, the psychological shift includes developing a tolerance for isolation and the potential monotony of long-term confinement. Human beings are inherently social creatures, and the prospect of extended isolation can be daunting. Preparing mentally for this involves establishing routines that provide a sense of normalcy and purpose. It also means planning for mental and emotional wellness through activities that stimulate the mind and spirit, from reading and games to exercises that maintain physical health. The discipline of maintaining these routines is crucial for mental resilience, helping to mitigate the effects of cabin fever and the stress of constant vigilance.

Moreover, the commitment to stay put, to bug in, requires a level of psychological fortitude and preparedness for scenarios that may test your resolve. This includes the potential of facing threats not just from the outside world but from within your own ranks—dealing with the stress, fear, and potential conflict that can arise in a group living in close quarters under high-stress conditions. Effective communication, conflict resolution skills, and emotional intelligence become as critical to your survival strategy as the physical fortifications of your home.

Preparing for long-term isolation also means coming to terms with the potential for significant lifestyle changes. This could involve rationing, adapting to a lack of modern conveniences, and finding sustainable ways to manage resources. The mental shift here is from a mindset of abundance to one of conservation and efficiency, always with the goal of prolonging your family's safety and security.

Finally, psychological preparedness involves embracing a proactive mindset towards learning and adaptation. The situation will likely evolve, presenting new challenges and requiring new solutions. This means being mentally prepared to adapt your strategies, learn new skills, and possibly even reevaluate your decision to bug in as the situation changes. It's about maintaining a balance between the confidence in your current plan and the flexibility to pivot as required.

In essence, the psychological journey from bugging out to bugging in is one of embracing stability over mobility, of finding security in the familiar while being prepared to adapt and overcome the challenges of isolation. It's a testament to the human capacity for resilience, requiring a deep well of mental strength, discipline, and the ability to find hope and purpose in the face of adversity.

When and Why to Choose Bugging In

Assessing Bug-In vs. Bug-Out

Assessing your situation is a critical first step in deciding whether to bug in or bug out, a decision that hinges on a multitude of factors each unique to your personal circumstances, geographical location, and the nature of the crisis at hand. This assessment isn't just a cursory glance over your current living conditions but a deep dive into the strategic viability of your home as a survival fortress in times of emergency. The decision to stay put or evacuate requires a comprehensive evaluation of several key considerations, each playing a pivotal role in crafting an effective survival plan.

Firstly, analyze the structural integrity and defensibility of your home. Consider the construction materials of your house—are the walls brick, which offers more resistance to external threats, or wood, which may require additional fortification? Examine the layout for potential vulnerabilities; windows and doors are primary entry points for intruders and must be evaluated for their strength and the feasibility of reinforcement. The presence of a basement or an attic could offer hidden storage for supplies or even a safe room in dire circumstances.

Next, the geographical location of your residence significantly influences the bug-in decision. Urban environments, while offering easier access to resources like food and medical supplies, also present higher risks of looting, vandalism, and other crime during widespread chaos. Conversely, rural settings offer isolation and potentially lower risk of human threats but might make you more vulnerable to being cut off from essential services and supplies. Proximity to natural water sources, elevation from flood plains, and distance from known fault lines or potential nuclear targets are crucial factors in this evaluation.

The availability and accessibility of resources play a critical role in your decision-making process. Assess your ability to stockpile necessities such as food, water, and medical supplies. Consider the sustainability of these resources; for instance, can you implement a rainwater harvesting system, or do you have space for a survival garden to supplement food supplies? The capacity to become self-sufficient is a significant advantage in favor of bugging in.

Community and family considerations cannot be overlooked. The presence of a strong, supportive community network can tip the scales towards bugging in, as cooperative efforts in fortification, resource sharing, and defense become viable. Family needs, particularly those of children, the elderly, or members with medical conditions, necessitate a stable, secure environment that a fortified home can provide.

Finally, evaluate the nature of the threat itself. Some scenarios, such as chemical spills or imminent natural disasters, may necessitate evacuation regardless of your home's fortifications. In contrast, situations where the threat is less immediate or localized, the security of a well-prepared home may offer the best chance for survival.

Through meticulous assessment of these factors, you'll be equipped to make an informed decision between bugging in or evacuating. This decision is dynamic, subject to change as circumstances evolve, requiring continuous reassessment and adaptability. Prioritizing the safety and well-being of your loved ones, the goal is to choose a course of action that maximizes your survival prospects in the face of uncertainty.

Environmental and Geographical Factors

Environmental and geographical considerations play a pivotal role in the decision-making process of whether to bug in or bug out. The specific characteristics of your location can significantly impact your ability to fortify your home and sustain a prolonged stay during a crisis. Urban and rural settings each present unique challenges and advantages that must be carefully evaluated to develop an effective survival strategy.

In urban environments, the dense population can be a double-edged sword. On one hand, the close proximity to resources such as supermarkets, hospitals, and hardware stores can provide a critical lifeline in the initial stages of a crisis. The infrastructure of utilities like water and electricity is also more robust, potentially offering a longer period of normalcy even as situations begin to deteriorate. However, the high population density increases the risk of social unrest, looting, and crime as resources become scarce. The challenge in urban settings is to create a secure, inconspicuous fortress that can withstand potential breaches by desperate individuals or groups. Reinforcing entry points, creating discreet storage solutions for supplies, and establishing silent communication methods with trusted neighbors can enhance urban survival prospects.

Contrastingly, rural locations offer the advantage of space and isolation, which can significantly reduce the threat of human conflict. The availability of land may allow for the development of sustainable food sources, such as gardens and small livestock, and the potential for setting up renewable energy sources like solar panels or wind turbines without the constraints of limited space found in urban areas. However, rural homes are often more vulnerable to being cut off from essential services. The distance from medical facilities and supply stores necessitates a higher degree of self-sufficiency and preparedness. Ensuring a reliable water source, such as a well or nearby stream, and having the ability to purify water is crucial. The geographical layout should be assessed for natural threats; homes in wooded areas may face risks from wildfires, while those near water bodies need to consider flood risks.

The decision to bug in also depends on the home's location relative to known natural disaster zones, such as hurricane paths, earthquake fault lines, or areas prone to flooding. Homes located within these zones require additional fortifications against the specific types of disasters they face. For instance, homes in flood-prone areas might need to be elevated, with critical supplies stored above potential water lines, while those in areas susceptible to wildfires may need defensible space cleared around the property to create a buffer zone.

When assessing the geographical and environmental factors of your location, consider also the routes available for evacuation should the situation necessitate leaving. Urban dwellers need to plan for heavy traffic and blocked routes, while rural residents should have multiple paths to avoid being trapped by natural obstacles or road closures.

In both urban and rural settings, the community's composition and your relationship with neighbors can significantly influence your bug-in strategy. A cohesive community can pool resources, share surveillance duties, and provide mutual aid, making a collective decision to bug in more viable. Establishing or joining a neighborhood watch program can enhance security and create a network of support during crises.

Ultimately, the choice between bugging in or evacuating is a complex one that requires a thorough analysis of your home's structural capabilities, the surrounding environment, and the geographical challenges specific to your location. By understanding these factors, you can tailor your preparations to create a secure and sustainable survival strategy that maximizes the natural advantages of your setting while mitigating its inherent risks.

Preparing Your Home for Bugging In

Initial Home Assessment

Evaluating your home's readiness for a bug-in scenario requires a methodical approach to identify both its strengths and vulnerabilities. This assessment is the cornerstone of preparing your home to serve as a secure survival fortress. Start by examining the **structural integrity** of your home. Check the foundation for cracks or signs of moisture that could indicate potential weaknesses. Assess the condition of the roof, looking for missing shingles or areas that may be susceptible to leaks. These are critical areas as they provide the basic shelter needed for survival.

Next, focus on the **windows and doors**. These are common entry points for intruders and must be scrutinized for their durability and the potential for reinforcement. For windows, consider the type of glass and frame material. Tempered or security glass and metal frames offer more resistance against break-ins. Inspect the locks on doors and windows, upgrading to deadbolts or adding additional locks where necessary. Reinforcement kits for door frames can significantly increase their resistance to being forced open.

The **perimeter** of your property also demands attention. A fence can serve as a first line of defense, deterring unauthorized entry. Evaluate the height and material of your fencing, and consider improvements or repairs to eliminate weak spots. Thorny landscaping around the perimeter can add an extra layer of natural security without drawing undue attention.

Surveillance and lighting are next on the list. Install motion-sensor lights around the exterior of your home to deter intruders and improve visibility at night. Consider the placement of security cameras, ensuring they cover all entry points and blind spots around your property. These systems not only act as a deterrent but also provide valuable information on the security status of your surroundings.

Internal security measures should not be overlooked. Secure any valuables in a safe that is bolted to the floor or wall. Create a designated safe room that can be fortified and stocked with essentials. This room should have reinforced doors, no windows or securely barred windows, and access to communication devices.

Assessing **resource sustainability** is crucial. Evaluate your ability to store and access water and food for extended periods. Identify areas in your home that can be used for bulk storage, ensuring they are cool, dry, and away from direct sunlight. Consider the potential for generating power through solar panels or backup generators, and assess the feasibility of installing these systems based on your home's orientation and local climate.

Finally, involve your **family in the assessment process**. Each member can offer unique insights into potential vulnerabilities and strengths within the home. Discussing plans and strategies not only helps in identifying overlooked aspects but also ensures that everyone understands their role in maintaining the home's security.

By meticulously evaluating these aspects, you can identify the necessary improvements to transform your home into a secure bug-in location. Remember, the goal is to create a living space that can withstand the challenges of a prolonged crisis, ensuring the safety and well-being of your loved ones.

Creating a Bug-In Plan

Materials
- Detailed maps of your local area and surrounding regions
- Contact list including family, friends, and local emergency services
- A comprehensive inventory of your home's supplies, including food, water, medical supplies, and tools
- Physical and digital copies of important documents (IDs, property deeds, medical records)
- A sturdy, lockable file or safe for storing important documents
- Notebooks and pens for documenting plans and inventory updates
- A whiteboard and markers for family briefings and quick updates

Tools
- Computer with internet access for research and digital document storage
- Laminator for protecting maps and important documents
- Fireproof and waterproof safe for document storage
- Software for creating and managing inventories (spreadsheet software like Microsoft Excel or Google Sheets)

Step-by-step instructions
1. **Gather Your Household:** Schedule a meeting with all members of your household to discuss the importance of having a bug-in plan. Ensure everyone understands the concept and the reasons behind it.

2. **Assess Your Situation:** Review the layout of your home, the local geography, climate, potential hazards, and resources. Consider factors like the likelihood of natural disasters in your area.

3. **Create Communication Plans:** Develop a plan for staying in touch with family members who are away during an emergency. Decide on a central contact person outside the immediate area.

4. **Inventory Home Supplies:** Conduct a thorough inventory of your current supplies. Categorize items into food, water, medical supplies, tools, and other essentials. Note expiration dates and quantities.

5. **Document Important Information:** Compile a document with important personal, medical, and financial information for each family member. Include contact information for emergency services and a trusted out-of-area contact.

6. **Map Your Local Area:** Use detailed maps to mark important locations such as hospitals, police stations, and potential resource points like grocery stores and pharmacies. Note evacuation routes and safe meeting points outside the home.

7. **Plan for Utilities:** Make plans for managing without utilities such as electricity, gas, and water. Include instructions for safely shutting off utilities if necessary.

8. **Secure Important Documents:** Place physical copies of all important documents in a fireproof and waterproof safe. Store digital copies in a secure, accessible online location.

9. **Assign Responsibilities:** Assign specific tasks and responsibilities to each family member according to their abilities. Include tasks like inventory management, security checks, and communication duties.

10. **Practice Your Plan:** Conduct regular drills to practice your bug-in plan, including communication drills, supply checks, and role-playing different scenarios.

11. **Review and Update Regularly:** Schedule regular reviews of your bug-in plan to update any information, replenish supplies, and make adjustments based on changing needs or circumstances.

Difficulty rating: ★★★☆☆

Safety tips
- Ensure all family members know how to use fire extinguishers and perform basic first aid.
- Keep important documents and maps in easily accessible locations for quick evacuation if necessary.
- Regularly check the condition of your supplies, especially perishable items and batteries.

Maintenance

- Quarterly, check the expiration dates on food and medical supplies, replacing any items that are close to expiring.
- Annually, review and update contact information, documents, and maps to reflect any changes.
- After each drill, gather feedback from family members to identify any areas of the plan that need improvement.

Common Mistakes and Avoidance Strategies

Overconfidence and Complacency

Overconfidence and complacency can be the Achilles' heel of even the most meticulously planned bug-in strategy. It's a common pitfall to feel overly secure within the confines of one's fortified home, leading to a dangerous underestimation of potential threats. This false sense of security can stem from several factors, including previous success in handling minor emergencies, a strong belief in the home's defenses, or simply the human tendency to normalize and become desensitized to risk over time.

The critical mistake in this mindset is failing to account for the dynamic and unpredictable nature of crises. Threats evolve, and what worked in past situations may not suffice for future emergencies. For instance, a home fortified against burglaries with standard security measures may not hold up against determined looters in the aftermath of a societal collapse, where the desperation of individuals can drive them to extraordinary lengths to access resources.

Minimizing risk by not continuously updating your bug-in plan and neglecting regular maintenance of security systems, supplies, and survival skills invites vulnerability. It's akin to leaving your flank exposed in a battlefield, providing an easy target for unforeseen challenges that can strike at any moment. The essence of military strategy lies in the constant assessment of threats and maintaining readiness to adapt, a principle that is crucial for civilian survival planning as well.

Staying vigilant and prepared for the unexpected requires a proactive approach. Regularly review and update your bug-in plan to incorporate new information, changes in your living situation, or advancements in technology that can enhance your home's security. This includes conducting periodic drills to ensure every family member knows their role during an emergency, inspecting and rotating supplies to prevent spoilage or degradation, and testing security systems and backup power sources to confirm they are in working order.

Moreover, continuous alertness involves staying informed about potential threats in your vicinity, whether they are natural disasters, economic downturns, or social unrest. This can be achieved by monitoring local news, maintaining communication with community safety networks, and participating in forums or groups dedicated to emergency preparedness. Such practices not only keep you aware of emerging risks but also foster a community of shared knowledge and support, which can be invaluable during crises.

Preparation, therefore, is not a one-time effort but an ongoing process of learning, adapting, and fortifying. It demands a mindset that respects the complexity and unpredictability of survival scenarios, recognizing that overconfidence and complacency are luxuries that can cost dearly in the face of real-world challenges. By embracing a strategy of continuous improvement and vigilance, you transform your home into a true survival fortress, capable of withstanding the tests of time and crisis.

Effective Communication Strategies

Effective communication is the backbone of any successful bug-in strategy, serving as a critical lifeline during emergencies. The importance of keeping communication lines open cannot be overstated, as it ensures that all members within the household are informed, coordinated, and ready to act in a unified manner when faced with crises. This section delves into the nuances of establishing and maintaining robust communication channels, both within the household and with the external world, to fortify your home against the unpredictability of emergencies.

Firstly, internal communication within the household necessitates a clear, predetermined plan that outlines who is responsible for what tasks during various types of emergencies. This plan should be discussed in detail with every family member, ensuring that even the youngest understands their role. For instance, designate who is in charge of securing food and water supplies, who manages medical needs, and who is responsible for maintaining the security perimeter of your home. Utilize tools such as walkie-talkies for instant communication within a larger property, ensuring that each family member has one on hand, with spare batteries readily available. Establish a central message board, physical or digital, where members can leave updates or notes regarding resource levels, security checks, or even morale boosters.

On the other hand, establishing external communication networks involves identifying and leveraging resources outside your immediate household that can provide assistance, information, or support during emergencies. This includes setting up reliable methods to receive updates on the situation outside, such as emergency alerts from local authorities or news from community networks. The use of HAM radios stands out as a particularly effective tool for external communication, capable of reaching far beyond the confines of your local area, even when other systems fail. To operate a HAM radio, at least one household member should obtain an amateur radio license, which opens up a vast network of emergency communication channels and information not accessible through conventional means.

Moreover, creating reliable outside communication links extends to digital platforms and social media, which can be invaluable for receiving real-time updates and for reaching out to emergency services or community help groups. However, it's crucial to have backup power sources for charging devices, such as solar chargers or battery packs, ensuring that your ability to communicate is not hindered by a power outage.

In addition to technological means, establish a network of trusted neighbors or nearby family members with whom you can communicate and coordinate for mutual aid. This can include sharing resources, providing updates on local conditions, or even forming a neighborhood watch program. Such networks not only enhance your security but also create a sense of community resilience that can be critical in times of widespread distress.

Lastly, it's essential to regularly test and practice your communication plan, just as you would a fire drill. This ensures that when an emergency does strike, every member of your household knows exactly how to communicate effectively, both internally and externally, minimizing confusion and maximizing the efficiency of your response.

By prioritizing communication as a cornerstone of your bug-in strategy, you transform your home into not just a physical fortress but a hub of coordination and information, significantly increasing your chances of navigating emergencies successfully.

Video BONUS

Chapter 2: Mental and Physical Preparedness

Developing the Military Mindset

Understanding the Military Mentality

The military mentality is built on a foundation of discipline, strategic planning, and an unwavering commitment to achieving objectives, principles that are equally vital in the context of civilian preparedness and home security. At the heart of this mindset is the understanding that preparedness is not merely an act but a continuous state of readiness. This readiness encompasses not just the physical aspects of security and survival but also the mental and emotional resilience required to face and overcome adversity.

Discipline, a cornerstone of military values, translates into the civilian realm as the rigorous organization and maintenance of your survival fortress. This means regular checks and updates to your home's security systems, consistent training in self-defense and emergency response protocols, and the disciplined allocation and rotation of food and water supplies. It involves creating a structured plan for bugging in that is meticulously followed and regularly updated to adapt to new threats or changes in your environment.

Strategic planning in a military context involves understanding the terrain, knowing your enemy, and utilizing your resources effectively. For civilian preparedness, this translates to a thorough assessment of your home's geographical location, including potential natural disaster risks and the proximity of external threats. It means mapping out your home's layout to identify vulnerabilities, strengthen defenses, and designate safe rooms. Strategic planning also involves understanding the capabilities and limitations of your household members, ensuring that each person has a role and knows how to perform it under stress.

The military mindset also emphasizes adaptability and resilience, qualities that are essential when bugging in. This means being prepared to modify your plans based on changing circumstances, whether that's a prolonged power outage, a natural disaster, or a societal collapse. It involves training yourself and your loved ones to remain calm and think clearly under pressure, using stress inoculation techniques similar to those used in military training. This adaptability extends to your physical fortress, ensuring that your home can withstand various threats through structural reinforcements, surveillance systems, and contingency supplies.

Leadership and teamwork are further aspects of the military mentality that apply to civilian survival strategies. Effective leadership involves clear communication, decisiveness, and the ability to inspire and motivate others. In a bug-in scenario, this means establishing a command structure within your household, where decisions are made swiftly and communicated effectively to all members. It also means fostering a sense of unity and purpose, ensuring that everyone is committed to the collective security and well-being of the group.

Finally, the military principle of "leave no man behind" translates to a commitment to the safety and security of every member of your household, including the most vulnerable. This means planning for the needs of children, the elderly, and pets, ensuring that your survival strategy is inclusive and comprehensive.

By adopting these military principles and integrating them into your civilian preparedness plan, you transform your home into a secure survival fortress. This approach not only enhances your physical security but also fortifies the psychological resilience of your household, preparing you to face any crisis with confidence and strategic foresight.

Cultivating Mental Toughness

Cultivating mental toughness is akin to reinforcing the foundation of a fortress, ensuring it can withstand the assaults of unforeseen crises and the relentless wear of prolonged stress. This resilience, deeply rooted in military training, is not innate but developed through deliberate practice and discipline. It begins with establishing a routine that challenges both the mind and body, pushing beyond comfort zones to foster a mindset accustomed to adversity. For instance, incorporating daily physical exercise not only builds physical endurance but also instills a sense of discipline and achievement. This could range from a rigorous morning run, regardless of weather conditions, to a structured workout regimen that includes strength training and cardiovascular exercises, each activity chosen for its ability to improve overall fitness and mental fortitude.

Discipline extends into daily tasks and responsibilities, emphasizing the importance of consistency and structure. It involves setting and adhering to a schedule that allocates time for work, training, family, and self-improvement activities, ensuring no aspect of personal or home defense preparedness is neglected. This might mean dedicating specific hours to the maintenance of home security systems, the organization of supplies, or the practice of self-defense techniques. The key is in the regularity and intention behind these actions, turning them into non-negotiable elements of daily life.

Focus, on the other hand, is sharpened through tasks that require attention to detail and concentration. Activities such as mapping out evacuation routes, strategizing defensive positions within the home, or even the meticulous planning of food and water storage are exercises in mental acuity. They demand a level of focus that, over time, becomes second nature, enabling one to make quick, informed decisions under pressure. To enhance this skill, one might engage in regular mental exercises such as puzzles, strategic games, or simulations of crisis scenarios, each designed to improve cognitive function and problem-solving abilities under stress.

Building mental strength also involves the practice of stress inoculation, gradually exposing oneself to controlled levels of stress to build tolerance and improve reaction to high-pressure situations. This can be achieved through simulations and drills that mimic potential crisis conditions, allowing one to experience the physiological and psychological responses to stress in a controlled environment. The objective is to familiarize oneself with these responses, understanding how to manage fear, anxiety, and decision-making when under duress. Techniques such as deep breathing, meditation, and visualization are invaluable tools in this process, aiding in the regulation of stress responses and the cultivation of a calm, focused mindset.

Equally important is the development of emotional resilience, the ability to maintain composure and optimism in the face of setbacks or when plans go awry. This involves a conscious effort to practice positive thinking, to learn from mistakes rather than be demoralized by them, and to view challenges as opportunities for growth. Building a support network of family and like-minded individuals who share a commitment to preparedness and resilience can provide emotional reinforcement, offering encouragement, sharing knowledge, and fostering a sense of community and collective strength.

In essence, cultivating mental toughness is a multifaceted endeavor that requires discipline, focus, and a proactive approach to personal development and preparedness. It is about creating a lifestyle that embodies the principles of resilience, adaptability, and strategic planning, ensuring that when faced with crisis conditions, one is not merely reacting but strategically responding with confidence and precision. Through consistent practice, reflection, and adjustment, mental toughness becomes an ingrained aspect of one's character, a fortress within, fortified against the uncertainties of the future.

Building Physical Resilience

Assessing Physical Fitness for Survival

Evaluating your physical fitness is a critical first step in building the resilience needed for effective survival in any scenario. This process begins with a thorough self-assessment, aiming to gauge your current level of fitness and identify specific areas that require improvement. The goal is to create a baseline from which you can develop a targeted fitness regimen that addresses your weaknesses and builds upon your strengths.

Start by conducting a series of **fitness tests** that measure cardiovascular endurance, muscular strength, flexibility, and body composition. For cardiovascular endurance, consider a timed run or walk, measuring the distance covered in a set period, or a step test to evaluate heart rate recovery. Muscular strength can be assessed through exercises such as push-ups, sit-ups, or squats, counting the maximum number you can perform in one minute. Flexibility tests might involve measures such as the sit-and-reach test, which gauges the flexibility of your lower back and hamstring muscles. Lastly, body composition can be assessed through methods like the Body Mass Index (BMI) calculation or more precise tools such as skinfold measurements or bioelectrical impedance analysis.

Upon completing these assessments, analyze your results against established fitness standards or consult with a fitness professional to understand where you stand. This evaluation will highlight areas needing improvement, whether it's building endurance, increasing strength, enhancing flexibility, or adjusting body composition. It's crucial to remember that each aspect of fitness is interrelated, contributing to your overall physical resilience and ability to handle the demands of a survival situation.

Developing a **personalized fitness plan** is the next step. This plan should be tailored to address the specific needs identified during your assessment, with clear, achievable goals and a structured timeline. For example, if you need to improve cardiovascular endurance, your plan might include regular running or cycling sessions, gradually increasing in intensity and duration. For strength, incorporating weight training or bodyweight exercises targeting all major muscle groups is essential. Flexibility can be enhanced through daily stretching routines, while body composition adjustments may require changes to both diet and physical activity levels.

Incorporating **variety** in your fitness routine is key to preventing boredom and ensuring comprehensive physical development. Mix different types of workouts to challenge your body in various ways and promote balanced growth. Also, consider the practical aspects of survival scenarios by including functional fitness exercises that simulate real-life activities, such as carrying loads, sprinting short distances, or navigating obstacles.

Monitoring your progress is critical. Regularly re-evaluate your fitness using the same tests conducted during your initial assessment. This not only tracks improvements but also helps in adjusting your training plan as needed to continue challenging your body and achieving new fitness milestones.

Recognizing the **importance of fitness** in survival scenarios cannot be overstated. Physical resilience enhances your ability to perform necessary tasks, from building fortifications to sourcing water or food, under physically demanding conditions. It also plays a crucial role in mental health, improving stress management, and maintaining morale in challenging situations. Fitness, therefore, is not just a component of survival but a fundamental asset that bolsters every aspect of preparedness and response.

By methodically assessing your physical condition, setting focused goals, and diligently working towards them, you transform your body into a tool primed for survival. This proactive approach to physical preparedness ensures that when faced with adversity, you have the strength, endurance, and resilience to protect yourself and your loved ones, embodying the principle that survival is not merely about enduring but thriving amidst challenges.

Developing a Survival Fitness Routine

Developing a functional fitness routine tailored to survival needs involves a strategic approach that integrates exercises designed to build strength, endurance, and agility, crucial attributes for any crisis situation. This routine should simulate real-life survival scenarios, preparing the body and mind for the physical demands of such events. The goal is to create a comprehensive fitness plan that not only enhances your ability to perform under stress but also ensures you can protect and provide for your loved ones in any situation.

Start by incorporating compound movements that work multiple muscle groups simultaneously, mimicking the actions you might need to perform during a bug-in scenario, such as lifting, carrying, and moving supplies or fortifying your home. Exercises like squats, deadlifts, and overhead presses are foundational movements that build overall strength. These should be performed with free weights, as they engage stabilizing muscles and promote functional strength, more applicable to real-world activities than machines. For those new to weightlifting, begin with bodyweight exercises, gradually progressing to using weights as strength and confidence increase. Ensure proper form and technique to prevent injury, possibly consulting with a fitness professional when starting out.

Endurance training is equally critical, as it prepares you to sustain effort over longer periods, whether that's enduring a prolonged crisis or performing labor-intensive tasks without fatigue. Incorporate cardiovascular exercises such as running, cycling, or swimming into your routine at least three times a week. Interval training, which alternates short bursts of intense activity with periods of rest, is particularly effective for improving both aerobic and anaerobic fitness, simulating the varied intensity of activities you might encounter during a survival situation.

Agility training enhances your ability to move quickly and efficiently, crucial for navigating obstacles or responding to unexpected threats. Ladder drills, cone drills, and short sprints improve coordination, balance, and reflexes, making you more adept at moving through varied terrains or confined spaces within your home during a lockdown.

Flexibility and mobility exercises are often overlooked but are vital for preventing injuries and ensuring your body can handle the demands placed upon it. Incorporate dynamic stretching into your warm-ups and static stretching into your cool-downs. Yoga or Pilates can also improve flexibility, core strength, and mental resilience, aiding in stress management and mental fortitude.

Your functional fitness routine should be structured yet flexible, allowing for adjustments based on your progress and any specific needs or limitations. A sample week might include three days of strength training, focusing on different muscle groups each day, two days of cardiovascular and agility training, and two days dedicated to recovery, involving lighter activities such as walking or flexibility exercises. Recovery is as crucial as the workouts themselves, allowing your body to repair and strengthen.

In designing your fitness plan, consider the resources available to you, such as equipment and space. Many exercises can be adapted to limited spaces or improvised with household items if traditional gym equipment is not accessible. For example, heavy bags of rice or water jugs can substitute for weights, and stairs can provide a platform for cardio and agility workouts.

Consistency is key to building and maintaining the physical resilience needed for survival. Set realistic goals, track your progress, and adjust your plan as needed to continue challenging your body and improving your capabilities. Remember, the objective is not just to survive but to thrive, ensuring you and your loved ones can face any crisis with strength, endurance, and agility.

Stress Management and Psychological Fortitude

Recognizing and Managing Stress

In the realm of survival, particularly when bugging in under crisis conditions, recognizing and managing stress is as crucial as securing water, food, or shelter. Stress, if not addressed, can impair judgment, reduce physical performance, and lead to conflict within the group. It's imperative to identify the signs of stress early, both in oneself and in others, to mitigate its impact effectively. Common indicators include irritability, difficulty sleeping, changes in appetite, feelings of overwhelm or anxiety, and physical manifestations such as headaches or stomach issues. Recognizing these signs is the first step toward managing stress under the pressure of a crisis.

Once signs of stress are identified, employing techniques to manage stress becomes paramount. One effective method is **deep breathing exercises**, which can be performed anywhere, anytime. This involves taking slow, deep breaths, inhaling through the nose for a count of four, holding for a count of four, and exhaling through the mouth for a count of four. This technique helps activate the body's relaxation response, counteracting the heightened state of arousal that stress induces.

Another technique is **progressive muscle relaxation**, which involves tensing each muscle group in the body tightly, but not to the point of strain, and then slowly relaxing them. Starting from the toes and working up to the forehead can systematically reduce tension throughout the body. This method is particularly useful for those experiencing physical symptoms of stress, such as muscle tightness or aches.

Regular physical activity is also a potent stress reliever. Whether it's a structured workout, a brisk walk around the perimeter of your property, or practical activities like chopping wood or gardening, physical activity can reduce stress hormones and stimulate the production of endorphins, chemicals in the brain that act as natural painkillers and mood elevators.

Establishing a routine can provide a sense of normalcy and control amidst chaos. This includes setting regular times for meals, sleep, physical activity, and even leisure or relaxation activities. A routine can help anchor individuals and provide a structure to the day, which can be particularly comforting when the outside world is unpredictable.

Communication plays a critical role in stress management, especially in a group setting. Establishing regular check-ins where each member can express concerns, fears, or simply talk about how they're feeling can significantly reduce stress. This not only helps individuals feel heard and supported but can also strengthen group cohesion and morale.

For those moments when stress becomes overwhelming, having a **pre-designated quiet space** where individuals can go to be alone, meditate, pray, or engage in any personal relaxation technique can be invaluable. This space should be respected by all members of the group, understanding that when someone is using it, they are taking necessary steps to manage their stress.

Lastly, **practicing mindfulness and meditation** can be incredibly effective in managing stress. Mindfulness involves paying attention to the present moment without judgment, while meditation can involve various practices, including focusing on a mantra, engaging in guided imagery, or practicing mindfulness. Both techniques can help shift focus away from stressors and promote a state of calm and relaxation.

Implementing these stress management techniques requires no special equipment or environment and can be adapted to suit individual preferences and needs. The key is to recognize the signs of stress early and take proactive steps to address it, ensuring that both you and your group can maintain mental and emotional resilience in the face of adversity.

Building Psychological Fortitude

Building psychological fortitude is akin to constructing an invisible armor around your mind, enabling you to withstand the pressures and uncertainties of prolonged crises with resilience and clarity. Developing this mental toughness involves a multifaceted approach, incorporating positive thinking, mental rehearsals, and a steadfast commitment to visualizing success despite adversity. The foundation of mental fortitude lies in the ability to maintain a positive outlook. This doesn't mean ignoring the reality of the situation but choosing to focus on what can be controlled rather than being overwhelmed by what cannot. To cultivate this mindset, start by identifying and challenging negative thought patterns. Replace thoughts of defeat or despair with affirmations of strength, adaptability, and perseverance. For instance, if faced with the thought, "This situation is hopeless," counteract it with, "I can handle this challenge through step-by-step problem-solving."

Mental rehearsals play a critical role in preparing for worst-case scenarios without succumbing to fear or anxiety. This technique involves vividly visualizing how you would successfully navigate challenges, from defending your home to ensuring your family's safety during a crisis. Spend time each day imagining yourself performing necessary tasks with competence and calmness. Detail every step, from securing your home's entry points to rationing food and water supplies, reinforcing the belief in your ability to manage and overcome difficulties.

Visualization extends beyond mere daydreaming; it's a strategic tool for embedding success into your subconscious, making you more adept at executing plans under stress. Picture the desired outcome in as much detail as possible, including the emotions you'll feel when you secure your home and protect your loved ones. This practice not only enhances mental preparedness but also boosts confidence and reduces the impact of stress on your decision-making processes.

Incorporating these strategies into your daily routine requires discipline and persistence. Begin by dedicating a few minutes each day to positive affirmation and visualization exercises. Gradually increase the time as these practices become a natural part of your mental preparedness regimen. Additionally, seek out resources such as books, podcasts, and workshops that focus on building mental resilience. Learning from experts and those who have successfully navigated crises can provide valuable insights and inspiration.

Remember, the goal of developing psychological fortitude is not to eliminate fear or uncertainty but to forge a mindset that can thrive amidst them. By embracing positive thinking, engaging in mental rehearsals, and harnessing the power of visualization, you equip yourself with the mental tools necessary to transition from merely surviving to strategically thriving during extended crises. This mental armor not only benefits you during emergencies but also enhances your overall quality of life, fostering a sense of inner strength and peace that permeates all areas of your existence.

Maintaining Morale and Motivation

Maintaining morale and motivation during prolonged emergencies is a critical component of psychological fortitude. The challenges of long-term crises can wear down even the most resilient individuals, making it essential to adopt strategies that uplift spirits and foster a positive environment. The key to sustaining high morale lies in recognizing the value of community, family support, and self-care, each playing a unique role in bolstering mental health and overall well-being.

Community engagement provides a sense of belonging and shared purpose, crucial during times of isolation or uncertainty. Establishing or joining a network of like-minded individuals who are also preparing for or navigating through emergencies can offer emotional support and practical assistance. Sharing knowledge, resources, and experiences within a community not only strengthens individual preparedness but also enhances collective resilience. Consider organizing regular virtual meetups or safe in-person gatherings with your community to discuss strategies, share updates, and motivate each other. This sense of solidarity can significantly boost morale, reminding everyone that they are not alone in their efforts.

Family support is another pillar of maintaining high morale. Involving family members in planning and preparedness activities can foster a cooperative spirit and ensure that everyone feels valued and understood. Create a family emergency plan together, assigning roles based on each member's strengths and preferences. Regularly practice drills and review your plans to build confidence and competence among all family members. Encourage open communication about fears, concerns, and suggestions. Acknowledging and addressing these feelings collectively can strengthen familial bonds and provide emotional comfort, which is indispensable during challenging times.

Self-care is equally vital in sustaining morale. The continuous demands of managing a crisis can lead to burnout if one neglects personal well-being. Develop a self-care routine that includes physical activity, healthy eating, adequate rest, and relaxation techniques such as meditation or deep-breathing exercises. Allocate time for hobbies or activities that bring joy and relaxation, whether it's reading, gardening, or crafting. Remember, maintaining your physical and mental health is not a luxury but a necessity for effective long-term crisis management.

In addition to these strategies, cultivating an attitude of gratitude can profoundly impact morale. Focus on the positives, no matter how small, and practice gratitude by acknowledging the things you are thankful for each day. This practice can shift perspective from what is lacking to what is abundant, fostering a more optimistic outlook.

Implementing these strategies requires intentionality and effort but remember, the goal is to create a sustainable way of living through prolonged emergencies. By valuing community, embracing family support, prioritizing self-care, and fostering an attitude of gratitude, individuals can maintain high morale, which in turn, enhances their capacity to navigate crises with resilience and strategic foresight.

Video BONUS

Chapter 3: Home Security and Fortification

Assessing and Strengthening Home Security

Conducting a Home Security Audit

To effectively conduct a home security audit, start by systematically evaluating the exterior of your home during both daylight and nighttime to identify potential vulnerabilities. Begin with the **perimeter** of your property. Check for areas where intruders could easily hide, such as overgrown bushes or dark areas that street lights do not reach. Consider installing motion-sensor lighting to illuminate these zones, using LED bulbs for their longevity and energy efficiency.

Next, assess all **entry points**, including doors, windows, and garage doors. Doors should be solid core or metal and equipped with deadbolt locks that extend at least one inch into the door frame. For windows, ensure they have locks and consider reinforcing them with security film that prevents glass from shattering. Inspect the condition of the frames and the glass itself for any signs of wear or vulnerability.

For the garage, ensure the door leading into your home is as secure as your front door and that the garage door is equipped with a modern, encrypted opener to prevent hacking. Evaluate the strength of your garage door itself and consider upgrading to a model designed for enhanced security if necessary.

Surveillance systems play a crucial role in home security. Evaluate potential locations for security cameras, focusing on entry points and areas of high vulnerability. Opt for cameras with night vision capabilities and motion detection. Ensure that your system is connected to a secure network to prevent unauthorized access.

Inside your home, assess the **security of personal valuables**. Consider a fireproof and waterproof safe bolted to the floor for storing important documents, jewelry, and small electronics. Evaluate the visibility of these valuables from outside to ensure they are not easily seen by passersby.

Smoke detectors and carbon monoxide detectors are essential for early warning in the event of fire or gas leaks. Test these devices monthly and replace batteries annually or opt for models with 10-year sealed batteries to enhance safety and convenience.

Conducting a home security audit also involves assessing your **family's emergency preparedness**. This includes having a clear, practiced evacuation plan, accessible emergency kits, and a communication strategy in case family members are separated.

For a thorough evaluation, consider using a **checklist** to ensure all areas are covered, and document any findings to prioritize improvements. Engaging a professional security auditor can also provide an expert perspective, especially for evaluating advanced security systems or identifying less obvious vulnerabilities.

Remember, the goal of this audit is not only to identify weaknesses but also to develop a **strategic plan** for addressing them. Prioritize actions based on the level of risk and potential impact on your family's safety. Regularly revisiting and updating your security plan is crucial as technology advances and potential threats evolve.

By meticulously assessing your home's security through a detailed audit, you lay the groundwork for creating a safe, secure environment that deters potential intruders and provides peace of mind for your family. Implementing the identified enhancements ensures that your home is not an easy target, reinforcing the safety of your loved ones and property.

Enhancing Entry Point Security

Enhancing the security of entry points is a critical step in transforming your home into a secure survival fortress. This involves a meticulous approach to fortifying doors, windows, and other potential access points to deter and withstand attempts at forced entry. Beginning with doors, the first line of defense should involve upgrading to **heavy-duty deadbolt locks** with a minimum 1-inch throw bolt. For added security, consider installing **grade 1 or grade 2 deadbolts** that meet American National Standards Institute (ANSI) specifications for strength and durability. Additionally, reinforcing the door frame and hinges with **3-inch screws** ensures that the door is anchored securely into the wall framing, significantly increasing resistance against brute force attacks.

For sliding glass doors, which are inherently vulnerable, the installation of a **charley bar** or a **patio door security bar** provides a robust physical barrier. These bars can be adjusted to fit the width of the door, creating a secondary locking mechanism that prevents the door from being forced open. Furthermore, applying **security film** to the glass can prevent shattering, a common method used by intruders to bypass locks. This film holds the glass together even when broken, obstructing entry and buying precious time during an attempted breach.

Windows, often overlooked in home security planning, require equal attention. Begin by ensuring all windows have **locks** and consider upgrading to **pin locks** or **keyed window locks** for enhanced security.

For ground-level windows or those accessible from a flat roof, installing **window bars or grilles** presents a formidable obstacle, though local fire codes and egress requirements must be observed to ensure safety in an emergency. Additionally, reinforcing windows with **security film** creates an invisible barrier that resists impacts and attempted break-ins.

Garage doors represent another potential weak point. Upgrading to a **smart garage door opener** that features encryption can prevent hackers from gaining access through your garage door. Securing the garage service door with a **deadbolt** and reinforcing it as you would the front door is equally important. For those with detached garages, ensure that the door leading into the home from the garage is as secure as the home's main entrance, employing the same strategies of deadbolts, hinge reinforcement, and door frame strengthening.

Surveillance and lighting play pivotal roles in entry point security. Install **motion-sensor floodlights** around the perimeter of your home to illuminate dark areas and deter intruders. Position **security cameras** to cover all entry points and vulnerable areas, ensuring they are visible as a deterrent but placed out of easy reach to prevent tampering. Opt for cameras with **night vision capability** and consider features like remote viewing to monitor your home's perimeter in real time from your smartphone or computer.

Finally, the psychological aspect of security should not be underestimated. The presence of **security signage**, whether from a monitored alarm service or even generic warnings about dogs or CCTV surveillance, can act as a significant deterrent to potential intruders. These signs should be prominently displayed at entry points and along the perimeter to maximize their effectiveness.

By methodically addressing the security of each entry point with these advanced locking systems, reinforcements, and deterrents, you significantly enhance the overall security of your home. This comprehensive approach ensures that your residence stands as a formidable barrier against threats, embodying the principles of military fortification in a civilian context.

Implementing Home Surveillance Systems

Implementing a robust surveillance and monitoring system is a cornerstone of modern home security, acting as both a deterrent to potential intruders and a means of gathering crucial evidence should a breach occur. The effectiveness of such a system hinges on strategic planning, selection of the right technology, and meticulous installation. To begin, evaluate your property's layout to identify key areas that require monitoring, such as entry points, perimeters, and any obscured zones that could serve as hiding spots for unauthorized individuals. This initial assessment should guide the placement of cameras and motion detectors to ensure comprehensive coverage without leaving blind spots.

Selecting the right cameras is critical; opt for high-definition models that offer clear images in a range of lighting conditions. Look for cameras with night vision capabilities to ensure around-the-clock surveillance. Cameras equipped with motion sensors enhance your security system by alerting you to activity in real-time, allowing for immediate response. Consider the benefits of both wired and wireless systems: wired cameras are less susceptible to interference and are ideal for permanent setups, while wireless models offer flexibility in placement and are generally easier to install.

When positioning cameras, aim for a vantage point that covers as much area as possible, ideally with a clear view of doors, windows, and gates. Mount cameras out of easy reach to prevent tampering, but within range of your Wi-Fi network if they require a connection. Ensure that outdoor cameras are weatherproof and equipped with protective casings to withstand the elements. For motion detectors, place them in strategic locations where an intruder would have to pass to access your home, such as pathways, driveways, and near entry points. Adjust the sensitivity settings to minimize false alarms triggered by pets or wildlife.

Integrating your surveillance system with an alarm system adds an additional layer of security. Choose an alarm system that can be linked to your mobile device, allowing you to receive alerts and monitor your home remotely. This setup not only acts as a deterrent but also enables you to respond swiftly to any security breaches by notifying the authorities or taking other appropriate actions.

For the installation process, carefully follow the manufacturer's instructions or consider hiring a professional to ensure optimal functionality and reliability. Regularly test your surveillance and monitoring system to identify and rectify any issues, such as camera obstructions or dead zones in motion detector coverage. Keep firmware and software up to date to protect against vulnerabilities and ensure your system benefits from the latest features and improvements.

Incorporating surveillance and monitoring systems into your home security strategy is a powerful way to protect your property and loved ones. By selecting the appropriate technology, strategically positioning devices, and ensuring regular maintenance, you can create a vigilant security system that deters potential intruders and provides peace of mind.

Building an Impenetrable Fortress

Fortifying the Perimeter

Materials
- Heavy-duty fencing material (e.g., chain link, wrought iron, or wood privacy fence)
- Barbed wire or razor wire (for topping fences, if legal in your area)

- Sturdy gates with reinforced hinges and locks
- Sandbags for creating barriers or reinforcing existing structures
- High-intensity outdoor floodlights
- Motion sensor lights
- Security cameras with night vision capability
- Alarm systems that can be triggered manually or by motion detection
- Signage for legal deterrence (e.g., "No Trespassing", "Beware of Dog")
- Landscaping materials (thorny plants, gravel for noise generation)
- Reinforced window bars or security film for lower-level windows

Tools
- Post hole digger or auger
- Hammer and nails/screws (appropriate for chosen fencing material)
- Wire cutters (for barbed or razor wire)
- Shovel for landscaping and sandbag placement
- Drill with drill bits (for installing window bars or security systems)
- Ladder (for installing lights and cameras at height)
- Staple gun (for securing wire or mesh)
- Wrench set (for tightening bolts on gates and fences)

Safety measures
- Wear heavy-duty gloves, especially when handling barbed or razor wire.
- Protective eyewear should be used during drilling, cutting, or any activity that poses a risk to the eyes.
- Use a dust mask when handling dry materials like sand or gravel to avoid inhalation.
- Ensure all electrical installations are done following local codes and preferably by a certified electrician.

Step-by-step instructions
1. **Assess your property's perimeter** to identify vulnerable points and areas that require reinforcement or coverage.
2. **Choose the fencing material** that suits your security needs and local regulations. Consider visibility, durability, and height.
3. **Install the fence** around the perimeter, ensuring it is deep enough into the ground to prevent easy removal or under-digging. Use the post hole digger or auger for deep, secure post placements.
4. **Top your fence with barbed or razor wire** if legal in your area, to deter climbers. Ensure it overhangs on the external side.
5. **Install sturdy gates** at entry points, reinforcing hinges and adding locks. Consider a keypad or electronic lock for added security.
6. **Position sandbags** strategically to reinforce fences or create barriers at vulnerable points.

7. **Install outdoor floodlights and motion sensor lights** around the perimeter to illuminate dark areas and deter intruders.
8. **Set up security cameras** to cover the perimeter, focusing on entry points and blind spots. Ensure they are out of easy reach and protected from tampering.
9. **Deploy alarm systems** that can be triggered by motion or manually in case of an attempted breach.
10. **Place signage** around the perimeter to warn against trespassing and indicate surveillance measures.
11. **Use landscaping as a deterrent** by planting thorny bushes beneath windows or along fences and spreading gravel in areas where an intruder might walk to create noise.
12. **Reinforce lower-level windows** with bars or security film to prevent easy entry.

Safety tips
- Always check local regulations before installing defensive measures like barbed wire.
- Regularly inspect and maintain your perimeter defenses to ensure they remain effective.
- Keep emergency numbers handy and inform household members about how to activate and respond to the alarm system.
- Practice caution when working with tools and materials, and consider professional installation for complex systems like electrical wiring or surveillance equipment.

Maintenance
- Periodically check fences and gates for signs of tampering, wear, or damage.
- Test security cameras and lights to ensure they are functioning properly and replace batteries or bulbs as needed.
- Inspect and replace any worn or damaged parts of your security system to ensure continuous protection.
- Trim landscaping features to prevent them from providing cover or aiding intruders.

Difficulty rating ★★★☆☆

Reinforcing Walls and Structural Elements

Materials

- High-impact resistant plywood or metal sheeting for reinforcing doors

- 3M™ Safety & Security Window Film for windows

- Sandbags for creating defensive barriers or reinforcing existing structures

- Expanding foam insulation for sealing gaps and reinforcing door frames

- Heavy-duty deadbolts and strike plates for doors

- Long screws (at least 3 inches) for securing strike plates and hinges

- Steel bars or grates for additional window protection

- Bullet-resistant panels (optional for high-threat scenarios)

Tools

- Drill with various drill bits

- Screwdriver set

- Hammer

- Nail gun (for plywood installation)

- Utility knife (for cutting insulation foam and window film)

- Measuring tape

- Caulking gun (for expanding foam insulation)

- Heavy-duty gloves

- Safety glasses

Step-by-step instructions

1. **Assess Vulnerabilities:** Walk through your home and identify weak points such as old doors, windows without locks, and areas with poor visibility.

2. **Reinforce Doors:** Replace the existing strike plates with heavy-duty versions and use long screws to secure them into the wall studs, not just the door frame. Install deadbolts if not already present.

3. **Install Safety & Security Window Film:** Measure each window pane and cut the security film to size. Clean the window surface thoroughly before applying the film, following the manufacturer's instructions for the best adhesion.

4. **Strengthen Door Frames:** Use expanding foam insulation to fill gaps around door frames, providing both thermal insulation and added rigidity against forced entry.

5. **Secure Windows:** For ground-level windows, consider installing steel bars or grates. Ensure they can be opened from the inside to maintain fire safety standards.

6. **Reinforce with Plywood or Metal Sheeting:** For doors and windows that need additional protection, cut plywood or metal sheeting to size and securely attach it over the door or window. This is especially useful for garage doors or back entrances.

7. **Place Sandbags:** For temporary reinforcement in anticipation of civil unrest or severe weather, stack sandbags around vulnerable points like ground-level windows and doors.

8. **Bullet-Resistant Panels:** In high-threat scenarios, consider installing bullet-resistant panels on doors and walls facing potential threat directions. These should be professionally installed to ensure effectiveness.

Safety tips

- Always wear heavy-duty gloves and safety glasses when working with tools and materials.

- Ensure modifications do not violate local building codes or homeowner association rules.

- Keep pathways clear to ensure quick exits in case of emergency.

- Regularly inspect and maintain all security enhancements for durability and effectiveness.

Maintenance

- Check the security film on windows periodically for peeling or bubbles, replacing as necessary.

- Inspect door reinforcements annually, tightening screws and checking for any signs of wear or damage.

- Clean and lubricate deadbolts and locks to keep them functioning smoothly.

Difficulty rating ★★★☆☆

Variations

- For aesthetic considerations, window grates can be custom-designed to match the home's exterior.

- In areas where sandbagging is frequently necessary, consider permanent landscape features that serve a similar protective function without the need for constant maintenance.

Installing Defensive Systems

Materials

- Reinforced steel doors with multi-point locking systems

- 3M™ Safety & Security Window Film Ultra S800

- Bullet-resistant fiberglass panels (UL Level 8)

- High-definition security cameras with night vision and motion detection

- Exterior-grade, high-intensity LED floodlights

- Smart locks with keypad, biometric, and remote access capabilities

- Acoustic glass break sensors

- Vibration-sensitive alarm systems for windows and doors

- Safe room kit including ventilation, communication systems, and reinforced door

Tools

- Electric drill with masonry and steel drill bits

- Heavy-duty screwdrivers (Phillips and flat-head)

- Tape measure

- Level

- Caulking gun

- Hammer drill for concrete installations

- Jigsaw or reciprocating saw for cutting bullet-resistant panels

- Wire strippers and crimping tools for security system installation

Safety measures

- Wear safety goggles and heavy-duty gloves during installation.

- Ensure electrical safety by turning off circuits when working on wired security systems.

- Use ear protection when using loud power tools.

Step-by-step instructions

1. **Upgrade Exterior Doors:** Remove existing doors and replace them with reinforced steel doors that feature multi-point locking systems. Use long screws to secure the door frame and hinges to the house framing.

2. **Apply Security Window Film:** Measure each window and cut the security film to size, leaving a slight margin for error. Clean the window surfaces thoroughly, apply a soapy water solution, and then place the film on the glass. Use a squeegee to remove bubbles and excess water.

3. **Install Bullet-Resistant Panels:** Measure the areas where bullet-resistant panels are needed, such as vulnerable windows or walls facing potential threat directions. Cut panels to size and secure them in place using a jigsaw or reciprocating saw for precise cuts. Fasten the panels securely to the wall studs or window frames.

4. **Set Up Security Cameras:** Choose strategic locations for cameras to cover all entry points and blind spots. Mount cameras using the drill and ensure they are out of easy reach. Connect cameras to your network and configure settings according to the manufacturer's instructions.

5. **Install LED Floodlights:** Identify dark areas around the perimeter of your home. Mount exterior-grade LED floodlights to illuminate these areas. Ensure lights are positioned to cover potential entry points without causing light pollution to neighbors.

6. **Upgrade Locks with Smart Locks:** Remove existing locks from doors and install smart locks that offer keypad, biometric, and remote access. Follow the manufacturer's instructions for installation and setup.

7. **Implement Glass Break and Vibration Sensors:** Install acoustic glass break sensors near windows and vibration-sensitive alarms on windows and doors. Connect these sensors to your home security system for immediate alerts.

8. **Safe Room Preparation:** Choose a room with no exterior walls for your safe room. Reinforce the door with a steel safe room door and install ventilation and communication systems. Line the walls with bullet-resistant panels for added protection.

Safety tips

- Double-check measurements before cutting or drilling to avoid costly mistakes.

- Regularly test security systems and backup power supplies to ensure they are operational.

- Keep a fire extinguisher accessible during the installation process in case of an accident.

Maintenance

- Inspect and clean security cameras and sensors regularly to ensure optimal function.

- Test smart lock batteries and replace them as needed.

- Check the condition of window security film and replace it if it shows signs of peeling or damage.

- Conduct a yearly audit of your home's defensive systems to identify any upgrades or maintenance needs.

Difficulty rating ★★★★☆

Creating Safe and Panic Rooms

Designing a Safe Room

Designing a safe room requires meticulous planning and attention to detail to ensure it serves its purpose effectively in times of crisis. The location of your safe room is paramount; it should be easily accessible to all household members while remaining discreet and difficult for intruders to find. Ideally, choose a central location within your home, such as a reinforced closet, basement, or an interior room with no windows, to minimize vulnerability. The goal is to have a space that is readily accessible without making it obvious to anyone with malicious intent.

When it comes to design, the structural integrity of the safe room must be your top priority. The walls, ceiling, and door should be constructed with reinforced materials capable of withstanding severe weather events and deterring forced entry. Consider using concrete blocks or steel panels for walls and a solid core or steel door with deadbolt locks. The door should swing outward to prevent being blocked by debris or forced inward by an intruder. Install a peephole or a small, bullet-resistant window in the door to safely identify visitors without exposing yourself to danger.

Ventilation is another critical feature that must be carefully integrated into your safe room design. An independent air filtration system can protect against smoke and biological contaminants. In scenarios where external air sources may be compromised, such as in chemical or biological incidents, having a sealed ventilation system with HEPA filters can be lifesaving. Ensure the system is powered by an independent energy source, like a battery backup or a manual power option, to maintain functionality even when the main power grid fails.

Communication tools are essential for staying informed and contacting emergency services. Equip your safe room with a hardwired telephone line, as cellular networks might be unreliable during emergencies. Additionally, include a battery-powered or hand-crank radio to receive updates. For added security, consider a two-way radio system capable of reaching emergency responders directly if traditional communication lines fail.

Stocking your safe room with supplies is the final step in ensuring its functionality. Store non-perishable food, water, and medical supplies sufficient for at least 72 hours. Include first aid kits, prescription medications, flashlights, extra batteries, blankets, and a portable toilet. Remember to consider the needs of all family members, including pets, when selecting supplies.

Incorporating these elements into your safe room's design creates a secure, fortified space that maximizes the safety and wellbeing of your loved ones during emergencies. By focusing on location, structural integrity, ventilation, communication, and supplies, you transform a simple room into a resilient sanctuary capable of withstanding various threats.

Constructing a Panic Room

Materials

- Reinforced steel door with multi-point locking system
- Bullet-resistant fiberglass panels (UL Level 8)
- Heavy-duty hinges and deadbolts
- Soundproofing insulation material
- Ventilation system with manual override
- Emergency lighting system (LED lights with battery backup)
- Communication devices (hard-wired landline phone, radio)
- First aid kit with emergency supplies
- Non-perishable food and water for at least 72 hours
- Fire extinguisher rated for electrical and chemical fires
- Portable toilet or sanitation supplies

Tools

- Electric drill with masonry and steel drill bits
- Circular saw or jigsaw for cutting panels
- Tape measure
- Level
- Caulking gun
- Screwdrivers (Phillips and flat-head)
- Hammer
- Wrench set
- Safety goggles
- Dust masks

Safety measures

- Wear safety goggles and dust masks when cutting or drilling to protect against flying debris and fiberglass particles.
- Ensure the room has adequate ventilation to prevent buildup of toxic fumes during construction and use.

- Install a carbon monoxide detector if the room will include any combustion-based heating or power sources.

Step-by-step instructions

1. **Select the Location:** Choose an interior room with no windows, preferably with only one door, located on the ground floor for ease of access during an emergency.

2. **Reinforce the Door:** Replace the existing door with a reinforced steel door. Install heavy-duty hinges and a multi-point locking system to prevent forced entry.

3. **Install Bullet-Resistant Panels:** Measure and cut bullet-resistant fiberglass panels to fit the walls, ceiling, and door of the room. Secure panels in place using screws, ensuring no gaps or weak points remain.

4. **Soundproof the Room:** Apply soundproofing insulation material to the walls and door to muffle any noise from inside the panic room. This can help keep your location hidden during a home invasion.

5. **Set Up Ventilation:** Install a ventilation system with a manual override to ensure fresh air supply without compromising the security of the room. Consider a system that can be closed off to protect against smoke or gas.

6. **Install Emergency Lighting:** Fit the room with an emergency lighting system that has a battery backup, ensuring visibility in case of power outages.

7. **Equip Communication Devices:** Place a hard-wired landline phone and a radio in the room to maintain communication with the outside world. Ensure these devices are always functional and within reach.

8. **Stock Emergency Supplies:** Fill the room with essential supplies, including a first aid kit, non-perishable food, water, a fire extinguisher, and a portable toilet or sanitation supplies. Regularly check and rotate these supplies to keep them fresh.

9. **Test the Room:** Once construction is complete, spend some time in the room to test all functions, including the door lock, ventilation, lighting, and communication devices. Make adjustments as necessary.

Difficulty rating ★★★★☆

Safety tips

- Regularly inspect the door, locks, and hinges for signs of wear or tampering.
- Test the ventilation system monthly to ensure it is operational and can be manually controlled.
- Check the battery life of all electronic devices and replace as needed to ensure they're always ready for use.

Maintenance
- Annually inspect the structural integrity of the bullet-resistant panels and the soundproofing material for any signs of damage or wear.
- Regularly update the emergency supplies, checking expiration dates on food, water, and medical supplies.
- Conduct a full functionality test of the panic room every six months, including door operations, communication devices, and emergency lighting.

Stocking Your Safe/Panic Room

Ensuring your safe or panic room is adequately stocked and equipped is a critical aspect of home security and fortification, directly impacting your ability to sustain through prolonged emergencies. The foundation of a well-prepared safe room lies in addressing basic human needs: water, food, medical supplies, and communication, each meticulously planned for long-term sustainability.

Water is paramount. Store at least one gallon of water per person per day, aiming for a minimum three-day supply but ideally extending to two weeks or more. Use durable, food-grade storage containers, clearly labeled and dated. Implementing a rotation system ensures freshness, with older containers used first and replaced regularly.

Food supplies should focus on non-perishable items that require minimal preparation, such as canned goods, freeze-dried meals, energy bars, and other nutrient-dense foods. Select items that cater to dietary restrictions and preferences of all household members. Regularly check expiration dates, rotating stock to maintain a fresh supply, and incorporate these items into your regular diet to ensure palatability and prevent waste.

A comprehensive **first aid kit** is essential, going beyond basic bandages and antiseptics to include prescription medications, over-the-counter remedies for common ailments, and specialized supplies for chronic conditions. Consider the inclusion of a first aid manual, as immediate medical assistance may not be available during a crisis.

Communication tools are crucial for both receiving updates and reaching out for help. A multi-powered radio (hand-crank and battery-operated) ensures access to emergency broadcasts, while a charged, durable cell phone with backup power banks keeps lines open to family and emergency services. A set of two-way radios can be invaluable for communication between family members if separated.

In addition to these essentials, consider the following to enhance your safe room's functionality and comfort:

- **Lighting**: LED flashlights and lanterns, coupled with ample batteries, provide reliable lighting without the risks associated with candles or oil lamps. Solar-powered or hand-crank options offer sustainability beyond battery life.
- **Sanitation**: A portable toilet, along with biohazard bags, sanitizers, and personal hygiene products, addresses waste management and personal cleanliness, critical in maintaining health and morale during confinement.
- **Tools and Repair Kits**: Basic tools (screwdrivers, pliers, a multi-tool, duct tape) can aid in minor repairs or adjustments within the safe room. A utility knife and scissors are also essential for opening packages and first aid.
- **Comfort Items**: Blankets, pillows, and sleeping bags provide warmth and comfort, reducing stress and aiding rest. Including books, games, or a battery-operated entertainment device can help pass time and maintain morale.
- **Security Measures**: While the primary function of a safe room is to offer protection, consider adding defensive tools that comply with legal standards and personal competence, such as pepper spray or a stun gun, for additional security.

By meticulously selecting and organizing these items, your safe room becomes a stronghold of safety and sustainability. Regularly review and update the contents, tailoring supplies to evolving needs and ensuring readiness for any emergency. This proactive approach transforms your safe room from a mere concept into a functional sanctuary, embodying the essence of preparedness and resilience.

Video BONUS

Chapter 4: Long-Term Food Storage

Principles of Food Stockpiling

Assessing Family Nutritional Needs

In assessing your family's nutritional needs for emergencies, the first step involves calculating the daily caloric intake required by each family member. This calculation is crucial as it directly influences the quantity and type of food you'll need to stockpile. Start by considering the basic metabolic rate (BMR) which varies according to age, gender, weight, and activity level. For an average adult male, the daily caloric intake ranges from 2,200 to 3,000 calories, while for an average adult female, it ranges from 1,600 to 2,400 calories. Children and teenagers, due to their growth demands and higher activity levels, may require different caloric intakes, often closer to the higher end of these ranges or even beyond, depending on their specific age and activity levels.

Once you've established a baseline for daily caloric needs, factor in the additional stress and physical demands that may arise during emergency situations. Increased stress levels, physical labor, and colder environmental conditions can significantly raise caloric requirements. Therefore, it's advisable to add an extra 10-20% to your baseline caloric estimates to account for these factors. This adjustment ensures that your stockpile can adequately sustain your family's energy levels throughout the duration of any emergency scenario.

Nutritional balance is another critical aspect of your emergency food stockpile. It's not enough to simply meet caloric needs; the diet must also provide a balanced intake of carbohydrates, proteins, fats, vitamins, and minerals. Focus on stockpiling a variety of foods that together meet these nutritional requirements. Carbohydrates should form the basis of your emergency diet, supplemented with adequate protein sources such as canned meats, beans, or protein bars, and fats from sources like nuts and seeds. Vitamins and minerals can be covered by including a range of canned fruits and vegetables, as well as multivitamin supplements to fill any gaps.

Tailoring your stockpile to meet specific dietary needs and preferences is also essential. Take into account any food allergies, intolerances, or special dietary requirements within your family. For instance, if a family member is gluten intolerant, ensure that your stockpile includes gluten-free alternatives. Similarly, for those with diabetes, focus on low-glycemic index foods to help manage blood sugar levels. The inclusion of familiar and preferred foods can also play a significant role in maintaining morale and normalcy during stressful times.

To customize your food supplies effectively, create a detailed inventory that lists the types and quantities of food you're storing, alongside their caloric and nutritional content. This inventory not only aids in ensuring a balanced and sufficient stockpile but also facilitates rotation and usage before expiration dates. Regularly review and update your inventory based on any changes in family size, dietary needs, or preferences, ensuring your emergency food stockpile remains aligned with your family's nutritional requirements.

By meticulously calculating caloric needs, ensuring nutritional balance, and customizing your stockpile to accommodate dietary preferences and requirements, you can create a comprehensive emergency food supply that supports your family's health and well-being in any situation. This approach not only provides the physical sustenance needed during emergencies but also contributes to psychological comfort and stability, reinforcing your family's resilience in the face of adversity.

Calculating Food Storage Needs

Calculating the quantity of food to store is a critical step in ensuring your family's safety and well-being during an emergency. The process involves a detailed analysis of several factors, including the number of people in your household, the duration of storage anticipated, and the caloric and nutritional needs of each individual. This calculation is not merely about stacking cans in a pantry; it's about strategic planning that incorporates both immediate needs and potential long-term scenarios.

Start by determining the number of people you're planning for and consider their age, gender, activity level, and any special dietary needs. An adult male, for example, generally requires about 2,500 calories per day, while an adult female may need about 2,000 calories. Children and teenagers have varying needs based on their growth stages. Remember, these are baseline numbers; in a survival situation, stress, increased physical activity, or cold weather can significantly increase caloric requirements.

Next, consider the duration of the emergency you're planning for. A common recommendation is to prepare for at least 72 hours, but given the unpredictability of many scenarios, aiming for a minimum of two weeks is prudent. For extended resilience, planning for one to three months or even longer can provide peace of mind and stability in the face of prolonged disruptions.

The type of food you store is equally important. Choose high-calorie, nutrient-dense foods that require minimal preparation and have long shelf lives. Grains, beans, canned meats, powdered milk, and dried fruits and vegetables are staples in long-term food storage for good reason. They provide essential nutrients and energy, are relatively compact, and can be stored without refrigeration.

When calculating food quantities, a practical approach is to create a daily meal plan that meets the caloric and nutritional needs of your household and then multiply by the number of days you're preparing for. This method not only ensures adequacy but also helps in maintaining variety and palatability, which are crucial for morale and mental health during stressful times.

Consideration must also be given to storage space and conditions. Food should be stored in a cool, dry place, away from direct sunlight and pests. Utilize airtight containers made of food-grade materials to protect against moisture and insects and to extend shelf life. Efficient use of space is key; think vertically and use shelving units to maximize storage areas.

Factor in emergency scenarios that could affect your access to food. Natural disasters, power outages, and supply chain disruptions can all impact your ability to replenish supplies. Having a diverse stockpile that includes ready-to-eat foods, ingredients for cooking simple meals, and seeds for growing fresh produce can mitigate these risks.

Finally, regular rotation of your food stockpile is essential. Incorporate stored food into your regular diet to ensure it's used before reaching its expiration date and replenish it with fresh supplies. This practice not only prevents waste but also familiarizes your family with the taste and preparation of your emergency food, making the transition smoother during actual emergencies.

By meticulously calculating your food storage needs and considering factors such as caloric requirements, storage duration, dietary preferences, and space limitations, you can create a comprehensive and reliable food stockpile. This preparation not only secures your family's nutritional needs during emergencies but also fortifies your overall resilience against unforeseen challenges.

Selecting Storage Containers and Methods

Selecting the right storage containers and methods for your long-term food stockpile is crucial to maintaining the quality, nutritional value, and safety of your food supplies. The integrity of your food storage directly impacts its effectiveness in sustaining your family during emergencies. Therefore, it's essential to choose containers and storage techniques that protect against common threats to food longevity, such as moisture, pests, light, and air.

For dry goods such as grains, beans, and flour, heavy-duty, food-grade plastic buckets with airtight lids offer an excellent storage solution. These containers are impervious to pests and can significantly reduce the penetration of moisture and air, two primary culprits in food spoilage. Ensure the buckets you select are made of high-density polyethylene (HDPE), marked with the recycling symbol #2, indicating they are safe for food use. For added protection, consider using Mylar bags as liners inside the buckets. Mylar bags, when sealed with oxygen absorber packets, create an oxygen-free environment that can extend the shelf life of dry goods for years. The process involves filling the Mylar bags, adding the appropriate size oxygen absorber, and then sealing the bags with a standard clothes iron or a hair straightener on a high heat setting. Once sealed, the bags are placed inside the HDPE buckets, and the lids are securely closed.

Glass jars with screw-on lids are another viable option for storing dehydrated foods, spices, and herbs. Glass is impermeable to gases and moisture, providing an excellent barrier to elements that might spoil the food. However, it's crucial to store glass containers in a dark, cool place since light can degrade the quality of food over time. Additionally, using vacuum-sealing attachments for jar lids can further extend the shelf life by removing air from the container, thereby minimizing oxidation.

For oils, syrups, and other liquids, consider using high-quality stainless steel containers with secure closures. Stainless steel is durable, does not absorb odors, and provides excellent protection against light. Ensure that the containers you choose are specifically designed for food storage and are not treated with any interior coatings that could interact with the food.

When storing food in any container, labeling is an essential step not to be overlooked. Use waterproof, permanent markers to clearly label each container with the contents, quantity, and the date of storage. This practice not only helps in organizing your stockpile but also in implementing a first-in, first-out rotation system, ensuring that older items are used before fresher ones.

In terms of storage methods, temperature plays a critical role in preserving food quality. A cool, dry, and dark environment is ideal for most stored foods, with temperatures ideally between 50°F and 70°F. Avoid storing food in attics or garages where temperature fluctuations are common, as this can accelerate spoilage. Consider using shelving units to keep containers off the ground, facilitating air circulation and making it easier to inspect and rotate supplies. Additionally, investing in humidity and temperature monitors can help you maintain optimal conditions for your food stockpile.

Implementing these storage containers and methods with attention to detail and foresight can significantly impact the longevity and quality of your emergency food supplies. By carefully selecting appropriate containers, utilizing effective sealing techniques, and maintaining optimal storage conditions, you ensure that your preparedness efforts provide maximum protection and sustainability for your family's nutritional needs during any crisis.

Best Foods for Long-Term Storage

Staple Foods for Energy and Balance

In the realm of long-term food storage, understanding and selecting the right staple foods are paramount for ensuring sustenance and energy for your family during extended periods of survival mode. The foundation of a well-rounded emergency food supply is built on grains, legumes, and proteins, each category offering unique benefits and essential nutrients vital for maintaining health and energy levels in challenging times.

Grains, such as wheat, rice, oats, and barley, are indispensable for their long shelf life and versatility. When stored properly in airtight containers and in a cool, dry place, grains can last for years without spoiling. They are a rich source of carbohydrates, the body's primary energy fuel, making them an essential component of any survival diet. For optimal nutrition, include a variety of whole grains like quinoa and millet, which are also high in protein and other nutrients.

Legumes, including beans, lentils, and chickpeas, are another cornerstone of long-term food storage due to their nutritional density and storage longevity. Rich in protein, fiber, and various vitamins and minerals, legumes not only offer a stable energy source but also contribute to a balanced diet by providing critical nutrients. They can be stored dry for years and rehydrated to nearly their original state, offering a versatile and nutritious option for meals.

Proteins, particularly dried or canned meats, fish, and poultry, are crucial for maintaining muscle health and overall bodily functions. Freeze-dried meats, jerky, and canned options like tuna, salmon, and chicken can last for several years and provide the necessary protein requirements. For those looking for plant-based protein sources, consider incorporating a variety of nuts and seeds, which also offer healthy fats and can significantly boost energy levels.

Diversifying your food stockpile is essential to ensure a balanced diet, especially during extended periods of reliance on stored food. This not only prevents nutritional deficiencies but also reduces meal monotony. Incorporate a mix of the above staples along with powdered milk for calcium, dried fruits and vegetables for vitamins, and honey or other natural sweeteners for an energy boost and flavor enhancement.

When selecting these staple foods, consider the specific dietary needs and preferences of your family. For instance, if someone has gluten intolerance, stock up on gluten-free grains like rice or quinoa. Similarly, for those with nut allergies, focus on alternative protein sources. The goal is to create a comprehensive food storage plan that caters to the health, energy, and taste preferences of all family members, ensuring everyone remains nourished and energized during times of crisis.

By focusing on these core staples and embracing the diversity within each category, you can build a long-term food storage system that not only sustains life but also supports a healthy and energetic family dynamic, even in the face of adversity.

Nutrient-Dense Foods for Health

Incorporating **nutrient-dense foods** into your long-term food storage strategy is not just about ensuring survival; it's about maintaining health and wellbeing during extended periods of self-reliance. The focus here is on selecting foods that are not only rich in essential vitamins and minerals but also capable of being stored for the long haul without losing their nutritional value. Dried fruits and vegetables stand out as prime examples of foods that retain a high concentration of nutrients post-dehydration. For instance, dried apricots are an excellent source of vitamin A, iron, and potassium, while dried spinach can provide significant amounts of vitamin K, magnesium, and iron. These foods offer the dual benefits of long shelf life and compact storage, making them ideal for maximizing the nutritional content of your food reserves.

When considering **supplements**, it's crucial to identify those that will best complement your stored food items by filling in nutritional gaps that may exist. A well-chosen multivitamin can serve as a nutritional safety net, ensuring that you receive an adequate intake of essential vitamins and minerals that might be harder to obtain during extended periods of isolation. Similarly, vitamin D supplements can be particularly important for individuals with limited exposure to sunlight, supporting bone health and immune function.

Omega-3 fatty acids, found in fish oil supplements, are another critical component for long-term health, supporting cardiovascular health and cognitive function. Given the potential difficulty in storing sufficient quantities of fish or obtaining omega-3s from plant-based sources, fish oil capsules present a viable and space-efficient alternative.

Protein powders, such as whey, soy, or pea protein, offer a concentrated source of high-quality protein, vital for muscle repair and growth. These powders can easily be incorporated into meals or consumed as shakes, providing a flexible and convenient protein source that complements the legumes and dried meats in your storage.

In selecting these nutrient-dense foods and supplements, it's essential to consider the specific needs of your household. For individuals with dietary restrictions or allergies, plant-based protein powders and gluten-free options can ensure that everyone's nutritional requirements are met without compromising safety or comfort.

Beyond the selection of foods and supplements, the manner in which these items are stored plays a significant role in preserving their nutritional value. Vacuum-sealed packaging and oxygen absorbers can extend the shelf life of dried fruits and vegetables, while cool, dark storage conditions are ideal for maintaining the potency of vitamins and supplements. Regular rotation of these items, just as with other components of your food storage, ensures that you consume them within their optimal freshness period, thereby maximizing their health benefits.

By strategically incorporating a variety of dried fruits, vegetables, and carefully selected supplements into your long-term food storage plan, you not only secure a source of sustenance but also ensure that your diet remains rich in the vital nutrients necessary for health and wellbeing during challenging times. This approach, emphasizing both variety and nutritional density, enables you to maintain a balanced and healthful diet, supporting both physical and mental health through periods of isolation or crisis.

Long-Lasting Packaged Foods

In the realm of long-term food storage, incorporating commercially prepared and packaged foods is a strategy that offers both convenience and reliability. These foods, designed for extended shelf life, can be a cornerstone of your emergency preparedness plan. The market offers a vast array of options, from freeze-dried fruits and vegetables to fully cooked meals that only require reheating. When selecting these products, it's crucial to consider factors such as nutritional content, packaging integrity, and ease of preparation.

Freeze-dried foods stand out for their lightweight and compact nature, making them ideal for storage in limited spaces. The freeze-drying process removes moisture from food, significantly slowing down the degradation process and preserving flavors and nutritional value. For instance, freeze-dried berries can retain their vitamin C content, providing essential nutrients even years after packaging. When choosing freeze-dried products, look for vacuum-sealed packaging to ensure minimal exposure to air and moisture, which can degrade the food quality over time.

Another category to consider is dehydrated meals, which often come in the form of soups, stews, and pasta dishes. These meals are typically reconstituted with boiling water, making them an easy option during situations where cooking capabilities are limited. Pay attention to the sodium content in these meals, as some can be excessively high, which could pose health risks during prolonged consumption. Opt for brands that prioritize natural ingredients and offer lower sodium options to maintain a balanced diet.

Canned goods, while heavier and requiring more storage space, provide a valuable source of proteins and vegetables. Look for cans with a BPA-free lining to avoid potential chemical leaching and opt for varieties with no added salt or sugar to keep your diet as healthy as possible. It's also beneficial to choose cans with pull-tab openings to ensure accessibility even without a can opener.

Incorporating ready-to-eat meals, such as those used by the military (MREs - Meals, Ready-to-Eat), can offer a practical solution for situations where cooking is not feasible. MREs are designed to be eaten without heating, providing a balanced meal with a shelf life of up to five years when stored properly. However, due to their high-caloric nature designed for active military personnel, it's important to consider your own dietary needs and activity levels to avoid unnecessary caloric intake.

While the convenience of pre-packaged foods is undeniable, there are drawbacks to consider. The cost of commercially prepared foods can be significantly higher than that of bulk-purchased staples. Additionally, reliance on these foods without proper rotation and consumption can lead to waste if products reach their expiration date unused. To mitigate this, implement a rotation system where older items are consumed first and replaced with new ones, ensuring your stockpile remains fresh and viable.

In terms of packaging, while many products boast impressive shelf lives, it's essential to store them in cool, dry places to prevent degradation. Exposure to extreme temperatures or moisture can compromise the integrity of the packaging and the food within. Regular inspection of your stockpile for any signs of packaging damage, such as swelling cans or compromised seals, is crucial to maintaining the safety and quality of your food reserves.

Ultimately, incorporating long-lasting prepared and packaged foods into your emergency food supply is a strategy that balances convenience with nutritional considerations. By carefully selecting products based on their nutritional content, packaging, and shelf life, you can ensure a diverse and reliable food stockpile that supports your family's needs during extended periods of self-reliance. Remember to complement these prepared foods with fresh, nutrient-dense options whenever possible to maintain a well-rounded diet.

Rotating and Maintaining Food Reserve

Establishing a Food Rotation System

Establishing an effective food rotation system is paramount in ensuring that your long-term food storage remains fresh, nutritious, and safe to consume. This system, often referred to as "First-In, First-Out" (FIFO), is a methodical approach that prioritizes the consumption of older items in your stockpile before newer ones. The implementation of a FIFO system not only helps in minimizing waste due to spoilage but also ensures that the nutritional value of the stored food is maximized, a critical factor in maintaining health and energy levels during extended periods of reliance on these supplies.

To initiate a FIFO system, start by organizing your food storage area in a manner that allows for easy access and visibility of all items. Use shelving units with sufficient space between shelves to accommodate different sizes of food containers and packages. Label each shelf by food category, such as grains, legumes, proteins, and vegetables, to streamline the process of locating and retrieving items. Within each category, further organize items by their expiration dates, placing those with the nearest dates at the front and those with the farthest dates at the back. This setup facilitates the natural selection of older items first, adhering to the FIFO principle.

For bulk items stored in large containers, consider dividing them into smaller, manageable portions using vacuum-sealed bags or airtight containers. Each portion should be clearly labeled with the packaging date and the estimated expiration date. This not only makes it easier to rotate stock but also helps in maintaining the freshness of the food by limiting exposure to air and moisture each time the bulk container is opened.

Implement a tracking system for your food reserves. This can be as simple as a handwritten inventory list or as sophisticated as a spreadsheet that details the types of food, quantities, packaging dates, and expiration dates. Regularly update this inventory as you add new items or consume existing ones. A well-maintained inventory not only aids in the rotation process but also assists in identifying the need for replenishing specific items, ensuring that your food stockpile remains balanced and sufficient.

Incorporate the practice of rotating food into your regular meal planning. This not only helps in gradually using up the stockpile but also familiarizes you and your family with the taste and preparation methods of stored food items, reducing the adjustment period in times of actual need. As you plan meals, prioritize the use of ingredients that are approaching their expiration dates, creatively incorporating them into recipes to ensure they are consumed while still at their peak quality.

Regularly inspect your food storage area for signs of spoilage or pest infestation, which can quickly compromise the safety and usability of your food reserves. Any compromised items should be immediately removed to prevent the spread of contaminants or pests to other stored foods. This inspection should be conducted at least monthly and more frequently in areas prone to high humidity or temperature fluctuations, which can accelerate spoilage.

By meticulously implementing and maintaining a food rotation system, you ensure the longevity, safety, and nutritional value of your food stockpile. This disciplined approach not only guarantees a reliable supply of food in times of need but also contributes to the overall preparedness and resilience of your household, aligning with the broader objectives of self-sufficiency and family protection.

Monitoring Food Quality and Shelf Life

Monitoring the quality and shelf life of your stored food is a critical aspect of maintaining a safe and nutritious long-term food reserve. Vigilance in this area ensures that your stockpile remains a reliable resource in times of need, safeguarding your family's health while minimizing waste. To effectively monitor food safety, familiarize yourself with the signs of spoilage and implement a systematic approach to inspecting your food supplies.

Firstly, understanding the signs of spoilage is paramount. For canned goods, watch for cans that are bulging, leaking, or have a rusted or damaged seal, as these are indicators of bacterial contamination and gas production, which can lead to botulism, a potentially fatal illness. With dry goods such as grains and legumes, signs of spoilage include mold growth, a musty or off odor, and the presence of pests or their droppings. These signs indicate that the food has been exposed to moisture or has been stored improperly, making it unsafe to consume.

For packaged and freeze-dried foods, discoloration, texture changes, and an unusual smell are red flags. Freeze-dried fruits and vegetables should retain their color and shape; any deviation from this could suggest moisture intrusion, leading to spoilage. Similarly, powdered products like milk or eggs should be free from clumps or an off smell, which could indicate moisture exposure or bacterial growth.

Implementing a regular inspection schedule is crucial for early detection of these issues. Dedicate time monthly to visually inspect each item in your storage, paying close attention to expiration dates and the condition of the packaging. Use a flashlight to examine the contents of cans and jars for any signs of discoloration or separation, which could indicate spoilage. For bulk-stored items like grains and legumes, use a scoop to check the product at different depths, as spoilage can occur from the inside out.

When inspecting your stockpile, always use gloves to protect against potential contaminants and to prevent the spread of spoilage from one item to another. If you encounter any food that shows signs of spoilage, it's imperative to dispose of it immediately and safely, ensuring that it's removed from your storage area to avoid contaminating other foods.

In addition to visual inspections, keeping an inventory log can be an invaluable tool in monitoring food quality. Record the purchase or packaging date, the expected shelf life, and any observations made during inspections. This log will not only help in tracking the age of your food supplies but also in identifying patterns or recurring issues with certain items or storage methods, allowing for adjustments to be made.

Replacing items as needed is a natural part of maintaining a long-term food reserve. When disposing of spoiled or expired food, take the opportunity to evaluate your stockpile's diversity and nutritional balance, replenishing it with high-quality replacements that meet your family's dietary needs and preferences. This continuous cycle of inspection and replacement ensures that your food reserve remains a cornerstone of your preparedness strategy, ready to provide sustenance and security in any situation.

By adopting these meticulous inspection and monitoring practices, you can confidently maintain a high-quality, long-term food reserve. This disciplined approach not only guarantees the safety and nutritional value of your stored food but also reinforces the resilience and self-sufficiency of your household, ensuring that you are well-equipped to face any challenges that may arise.

Using Stockpiled Food in Daily Meals

Incorporating stockpiled food into daily meals is a strategic approach that not only maximizes the utility of your reserves but also ensures your family is accustomed to the taste and preparation methods of your stored supplies. This practice is essential for minimizing waste and ensuring that your stockpile remains fresh and viable for when you truly need it. To seamlessly integrate stockpiled food into your daily cooking routines, consider the following detailed strategies and tips.

Firstly, familiarize yourself with the nutritional content and cooking requirements of your stored foods. Grains such as rice, quinoa, and barley serve as versatile bases for a variety of dishes, from hearty breakfasts to satisfying dinners. Understanding that beans and legumes can be soaked overnight to reduce cooking time makes them more accessible for use in daily meals. For proteins, freeze-dried meats can be rehydrated and added to soups, stews, and casseroles, providing essential nutrients and variety to your diet.

Creating a meal plan that incorporates stockpiled ingredients is a practical next step. This plan should outline weekly meals, utilizing ingredients that are closest to their expiration date first. For example, if you have a surplus of canned tomatoes and dried pasta, consider preparing a tomato-based pasta dish. If there are powdered eggs and freeze-dried vegetables nearing their use-by date, they can be used to make a nutritious breakfast scramble. The key is to blend stockpiled items with fresh ingredients to maintain a balanced diet, ensuring that meals are both nutritious and enjoyable.

Adapting recipes to include stockpiled foods is simpler than it may seem. Many recipes are forgiving and can accommodate substitutions. Dried or powdered milk can replace fresh milk in baking recipes, and canned chicken can be used instead of fresh in chicken salads or sandwiches. When using dried beans or legumes, remember to account for the increased volume after soaking and cooking when substituting them for canned varieties in recipes.

To ensure variety and prevent palate fatigue, get creative with spices and seasonings. The strategic use of herbs, spices, and condiments can transform the taste of stockpiled foods, making them more appealing. Experiment with different flavor profiles to keep meals interesting and diverse. For instance, adding a blend of Mediterranean spices to canned beans can give them a fresh and vibrant flavor, suitable for inclusion in salads or as a side dish.

Another effective strategy is to practice batch cooking with stockpiled ingredients. Preparing large quantities of meals such as chili, soups, or casseroles that incorporate your stored foods can save time and energy. These meals can be consumed over several days or frozen for future use, ensuring that your stockpile is being rotated and consumed before items expire. This practice not only makes efficient use of your reserves but also familiarizes your family with the taste and texture of stockpiled food, making the transition smoother in times of need.

Incorporating stockpiled food into daily meals requires a shift in mindset, viewing your reserves not just as emergency rations but as an integral part of your regular diet. This approach not only ensures that your stockpile remains fresh and ready for emergencies but also promotes a sustainable lifestyle that minimizes waste and maximizes resources. By adopting these strategies, you can effectively use your stored food in everyday cooking, ensuring your family is well-fed, prepared, and adaptable, regardless of the circumstances.

Video BONUS

Would you like to listen to this book?

Scan the QrCode below and download the
Audio Version

Chapter 5: Water Security and Purification

Securing a Reliable Water Supply

Assessing Household Water Needs

To accurately assess the water needs for your household, it's essential to calculate the daily water requirements with precision, factoring in drinking, cooking, and hygiene. Each member of your household will require, on average, about half a gallon of water per day for drinking alone. However, when you account for cooking and hygiene, this amount can quickly escalate to approximately 1 to 1.5 gallons per person per day.

Begin by calculating the total amount of water your household consumes on a typical day. This includes all water used for cooking, cleaning, personal hygiene, pets, and plants. For cooking and drinking, prioritize the use of clean, purified water. For hygiene purposes, such as bathing and flushing toilets, slightly lower quality water can be considered acceptable, though safety should never be compromised.

In emergency scenarios, water usage patterns can drastically change. It's prudent to plan for increased consumption due to stress, higher physical activity levels, or the need for additional hygiene practices. Therefore, adding a buffer of 20% to your daily water consumption estimate can provide a more realistic figure for emergency planning.

Special needs within the household must also be considered. For example, infants or individuals with certain health conditions may require additional water or specific water treatment to ensure safety. Similarly, if a family member is pregnant or nursing, their water intake needs increase.

For a family of four, the baseline calculation for daily water needs would be approximately 4 to 6 gallons per day under normal conditions. However, with the added 20% buffer for emergencies and accounting for special needs, this estimate could rise to 8 gallons per day or more.

To ensure you're prepared for various scenarios, including possible disruptions in water supply, it's advisable to store at least a two-week supply of water at all times. This means, for a family of four, aiming for a minimum storage of 112 gallons of water. This volume provides a comfortable margin for drinking, cooking, and basic hygiene needs during an extended emergency situation.

When planning your water storage, consider using food-grade water storage containers that are specifically designed to keep water safe from contamination. Regularly rotate your water supply every six months to maintain freshness, marking the storage date on each container. For households with limited space, innovative solutions such as bathtub liners designed for emergency water storage can provide a significant amount of water without requiring additional space.

Remember, assessing your household's water needs is not a one-time task. Reevaluate your water strategy periodically, especially as your family's needs and circumstances evolve. By taking a detailed and proactive approach to water planning, you ensure that in any crisis, your loved ones remain hydrated, healthy, and prepared.

Identifying Local Water Sources

Identifying local water sources is a critical step in ensuring a reliable supply for your household, especially in scenarios where conventional water systems may be compromised. This process involves a thorough evaluation of natural water sources such as rivers, lakes, and wells within your vicinity, as well as an assessment of the reliability and safety of municipal water systems during crises. To effectively secure a sustainable water source, it's essential to understand the specific considerations and methods for evaluating each type of water source.

For natural water sources like rivers and lakes, the first step is to map out their locations in relation to your home. Utilize online resources, local government data, and topographical maps to identify the closest bodies of water. Once identified, it's crucial to assess the quality of these water sources. Look for clear, flowing water rather than stagnant or cloudy water, as moving water is less likely to harbor pathogens and contaminants. However, even the clearest stream can contain invisible biological and chemical hazards. Therefore, collecting samples for testing is a wise move. Many county extension offices offer water testing services, or you can purchase home testing kits designed to detect common contaminants such as bacteria, nitrates, and heavy metals.

Wells present a more controlled but equally variable water source. If you have access to a well, understanding its depth, recharge rate, and water quality becomes paramount. Deep wells typically offer cleaner water than shallow ones, but they require a reliable pump system for extraction. Regular testing for contaminants is also recommended for well owners, with particular attention to changes in water taste, color, or odor, which can indicate contamination.

Turning to municipal water systems, while these are designed to be reliable and safe, emergencies such as natural disasters or infrastructure failures can compromise water quality and availability. Familiarize yourself with your local water utility's emergency response plan and water quality reports, usually available on their website. This information can provide insight into the system's vulnerabilities and help you plan accordingly. Additionally, consider installing a water storage system that can be filled in anticipation of an emergency, ensuring you have an uncontaminated supply should the municipal system fail.

Safety concerns with public water systems during crises include contamination from broken pipes, flooding, or treatment failures. In such events, water advisories or boil orders may be issued. Stay informed through local news outlets, government websites, and direct alerts from your water utility. Having a plan for purifying and filtering water is essential. Basic methods include boiling, chemical disinfection with household bleach, and using portable water filters designed to remove pathogens.

In summary, securing a reliable water supply involves a multifaceted approach that includes identifying potential local water sources, assessing their safety and reliability, and being prepared to treat water as needed. By taking these steps, you can ensure that you and your loved ones have access to safe drinking water, even in the most challenging circumstances.

Rainwater Harvesting System Setup

Rainwater harvesting is a practical and efficient method to secure a supplementary water supply for your household, especially in times of emergency or when traditional water sources become unreliable. The process involves collecting rainwater from surfaces such as roofs and then storing it for future use. To set up an effective rainwater harvesting system, you'll need to consider several key factors, including the collection surface, storage solutions, and filtration methods, as well as being mindful of legal requirements and guidelines that govern rainwater harvesting in your area.

Firstly, identify a suitable collection surface, typically your home's roof. Roofs made of metal, slate, or tiles are preferable due to their smooth surfaces, which minimize contaminants and facilitate easier water collection. Avoid roofs with toxic materials, such as asbestos shingles, or those treated with pesticides or preservative coatings, as they can leach harmful substances into the collected water. Install guttering and downspouts around the perimeter of the roof if they're not already in place. Ensure these components are made of high-quality, durable materials such as PVC or aluminum to withstand weather conditions and the weight of water over time. Use leaf screens or gutter guards to prevent debris from entering the system, which can reduce maintenance and improve water quality.

For storage, select food-grade, UV-resistant water storage tanks to prevent algae growth and plastic degradation. The size of the tank will depend on your roof area and the average rainfall in your region. A general rule is that 1,000 square feet of roof can collect approximately 600 gallons of water from 1 inch of rainfall. Therefore, adjust your storage capacity based on your collection potential and water needs. Place the tank on a solid foundation, such as a concrete pad, and ensure it's elevated above ground level to facilitate gravity-fed water flow. This setup allows for easier distribution of the collected water without the need for pumps, saving energy and reducing complexity.

Incorporating a first-flush diverter is crucial for improving water quality. This device diverts the initial flow of rainwater, which carries most of the contaminants from the roof and gutters, away from the storage tank. After the first flush of water is diverted, cleaner water is then directed into the storage tank. The volume of water to be diverted can be calculated based on the roof area and the level of debris typically encountered, with common systems diverting the first 10-15 gallons of water from each rainfall event.

Before using the harvested rainwater, especially for drinking, it must be properly filtered and disinfected. Basic filtration can be achieved with a sediment filter to remove particles, followed by a carbon filter to improve taste and odor. For potable applications, further purification is necessary, typically through UV light treatment or chlorination, to eliminate pathogens.

Regarding legal considerations, it's essential to check local regulations and guidelines before setting up a rainwater harvesting system. Some jurisdictions may require permits, especially for large systems or those used for potable water. Additionally, certain areas might have restrictions on rainwater usage due to water rights laws. Contact your local water authority or environmental agency to ensure compliance with all regulations and to register your system if required.

By meticulously planning and implementing your rainwater harvesting system with attention to these details, you can establish a reliable, sustainable water source that enhances your household's resilience and self-sufficiency. Remember, the success of your system hinges not only on its design and installation but also on regular maintenance, including cleaning gutters, inspecting tanks, and replacing filters to ensure the quality and safety of your water supply.

Storage Solutions for Long-Term Use

Choosing Water Storage Containers

Selecting the appropriate water storage containers is a critical step in ensuring the safety and longevity of your water supply. The choice of container can significantly impact the water's quality over time, making it essential to understand the pros and cons of various materials and designs available. When it comes to storing water for long-term use, the primary considerations should include the container's material, capacity, durability, and the safety of the water stored within.

Plastic barrels, often made from high-density polyethylene (HDPE), are a popular choice for water storage due to their lightweight nature, resistance to impact, and affordability. HDPE is a food-grade plastic that does not leach chemicals into the water, making it safe for long-term storage. These barrels typically come in sizes ranging from 15 to 55 gallons, making them versatile for different needs and spaces. When choosing plastic barrels, look for those marked with a "food-grade" label or the number 2 inside the recycle symbol, indicating they are made from HDPE. It's also crucial to ensure these barrels have not previously been used to store chemicals or non-food items, as residues can contaminate your water supply.

Glass containers offer an alternative to plastic, with the advantage of being chemically inert, meaning they will not impart any taste or odor to the water. They are also impermeable to gases and vapors, ensuring the water remains pure. However, glass is heavy and fragile, making it less practical for large quantities of water or situations where the container may need to be moved frequently. For small-scale, personal water storage, glass can be an excellent choice, particularly if stored in a stable, protected environment where breakage risk is minimal.

Metal tanks, specifically those made from stainless steel, present a durable and long-lasting option for water storage. Stainless steel is resistant to corrosion, does not leach contaminants into the water, and can withstand a wide range of temperatures. These tanks are ideal for large-scale water storage needs, such as whole-house systems or outdoor collection systems. When selecting a metal tank, it's important to choose food-grade stainless steel and ensure the tank is designed specifically for water storage, as some metal tanks are intended for other uses and may contain coatings or materials unsuitable for potable water.

Regardless of the material chosen, all water storage containers should offer protection against UV light to prevent algae growth and water degradation. Containers intended for outdoor use should be either naturally resistant to UV light, like certain plastics and metals, or painted with a UV-resistant coating. Additionally, the container should have a secure, airtight lid to prevent contamination from insects, dust, and other environmental pollutants.

In terms of capacity, the size of the container should match your calculated water needs, taking into account the number of people in your household and the intended use of the stored water. It's often advisable to have a variety of sizes to accommodate different situations, such as portable containers for evacuation scenarios and larger tanks for stationary, long-term storage.

To ensure the highest safety and longevity of your water supply, regular maintenance of your storage containers is essential. This includes cleaning and sanitizing the containers before the initial use and periodically inspecting them for signs of wear, damage, or contamination. For plastic and metal containers, use a solution of unscented bleach and water to sanitize, followed by thorough rinsing with clean water. Glass containers can be cleaned with hot, soapy water, rinsed well, and then sanitized with a bleach solution if desired.

By carefully selecting the right water storage containers and maintaining them properly, you can secure a safe and reliable water supply for your household, ensuring preparedness for any situation.

Short vs. Long-Term Water Storage

In addressing the critical aspect of water storage, it's essential to differentiate between short-term and long-term needs, as each requires a distinct approach and preparation. For short-term water storage, aimed at covering up to 72 hours, the focus is on immediate accessibility and portability. Utilizing commercially available bottled water is a practical option, as these are typically sealed, purified, and ready for immediate use. For those preferring to prepare their own containers, food-grade polyethylene plastic containers, marked with a recycling symbol #1, #2, or #4, ensure safety and non-contamination of the water. These containers should be filled with tap water and stored in a cool, dark place to prevent bacterial growth. It's advisable to rotate this water supply every six months, ensuring its freshness and potability.

Transitioning to long-term water storage, the strategies evolve to accommodate the need for sustainability over months to years. Here, larger, more durable containers are necessary. Fifty-five-gallon food-grade barrels, made of either high-density polyethylene (HDPE) or blue polyethylene, are widely recommended for their durability and safety. These barrels should be filled with chlorinated municipal water, and if the water is from a non-chlorinated source, adding unscented household bleach—specifically, eight drops per gallon—ensures purification. Placement of these barrels is crucial; they should rest on wooden pallets, keeping them off direct contact with concrete or the ground to prevent any potential chemical reactions that could compromise the water quality. For long-term storage, the water should be treated with water preservatives, available commercially, which can extend the potability of the water for up to five years, eliminating the need for frequent rotation.

Moreover, integrating a multi-barrier approach to water purification for long-term storage enhances safety. This includes pre-filtering to remove sediments, chemical treatment to kill pathogens, and boiling or distillation before consumption. For households aiming for self-sufficiency, investing in a high-quality, gravity-fed water filtration system capable of purifying rainwater or water from natural sources adds an additional layer of security and independence.

In both short-term and long-term water storage strategies, meticulous attention to the containers' integrity is paramount. Regular inspection for leaks, cracks, or contamination is essential, with immediate action taken to replace compromised containers. Additionally, labeling each container with the date of storage helps manage rotation and ensures the oldest water is used first, maintaining a cycle of fresh supply.

Incorporating these detailed strategies into your preparedness plan guarantees that whether facing a brief disruption or a prolonged period of self-reliance, your water needs are securely met. By adopting specific materials, tools, and techniques tailored to the duration of storage, you ensure the safety, accessibility, and sustainability of your water supply, a cornerstone of comprehensive emergency preparedness.

Preventing Water Contamination

Ensuring the safety of your stored water involves a multi-faceted approach, focusing on preventing contamination right from the collection point to the storage and eventual use. The integrity of your water supply hinges on meticulous attention to both the physical and chemical properties of the storage environment, as well as the procedural aspects of handling water. To keep your stored water clean and safe, it's essential to implement a series of best practices designed to mitigate the risk of contamination at every step of the process.

Firstly, the cleanliness of the containers prior to water storage cannot be overstated. Using a solution of unscented bleach diluted with water, scrub the insides of your containers thoroughly to eliminate any residues or contaminants that could spoil the stored water. Rinse these containers several times with clean water to ensure no traces of bleach remain. This initial step is crucial for establishing a sterile environment for water storage.

Once the containers are prepared, the next line of defense against contamination is the method of filling these containers. Ensure that the water being stored has been treated or comes from a clean, reliable source. If you're filling containers from a tap or municipal source, let the water run for a few minutes first to flush any stagnant water from the pipes. When transferring water to the storage container, use a clean funnel or hose that has been sterilized with a bleach solution, and make sure the exterior of the container does not come into contact with unclean surfaces or the ground.

After the water is stored, the placement of your containers plays a pivotal role in maintaining water quality. Store containers in a cool, dark place away from direct sunlight to prevent the growth of algae and bacteria. UV light can degrade certain types of plastic containers over time, which can lead to leaching of chemicals into the water. Additionally, avoid placing containers near chemicals, fuels, or toxic substances, as vapors can permeate plastic containers, contaminating the water with harmful substances.

Regular inspection of stored water is a critical aspect of maintaining its safety. Every few months, visually inspect the water for any signs of algae growth or sedimentation. Smell the water for any unusual odors that could indicate bacterial growth or contamination. If any containers show signs of compromise, such as leaks, cracks, or contamination, the water should be disposed of, and the container either thoroughly cleaned and re-sanitized or replaced.

The role of airtight seals cannot be underestimated in preventing contamination. Ensure that all containers are sealed with tight-fitting lids that prevent the ingress of contaminants. For added protection, you can seal the lid edges with tamper-evident tape, which also serves as an indicator if the container has been opened or tampered with. This practice is particularly important if the water is to be stored for an extended period or in locations accessible to children or animals.

Finally, the concept of water rotation should be ingrained in your long-term storage strategy. Even properly stored water should be used and replaced on a regular basis, ideally every six to twelve months. This rotation ensures the water remains fresh and reduces the risk of chemical degradation of the container that could lead to contamination. When rotating your water supply, use the oldest stored water first, following the principle of first-in, first-out.

Implementing these best practices requires diligence and a commitment to maintaining the highest standards of hygiene and safety in water storage. By adhering to these guidelines, you can ensure that your stored water remains clean, safe, and ready for use whenever the need arises, safeguarding the health and well-being of you and your loved ones.

Purification Techniques for Safe Water

Understanding Water Contaminants

Water, the essence of life, can also harbor dangers that compromise its safety and the health of those who consume it. Understanding common water contaminants is crucial for ensuring a safe drinking supply, especially in scenarios where traditional water treatment facilities are not operational. Contaminants in water can be broadly categorized into biological, chemical, and physical types, each presenting unique threats to water quality and, consequently, to human health.

Biological contaminants, also known as pathogens, include bacteria, viruses, parasites, and protozoa. These microorganisms can originate from human and animal waste contaminating water sources through sewage overflows, agricultural runoff, and untreated waste. Diseases such as cholera, giardiasis, and hepatitis can arise from consuming water tainted with these pathogens. Ensuring water is properly boiled or disinfected with chlorine-based products or ultraviolet light can mitigate the risk posed by biological contaminants.

Chemical contaminants encompass a wide range of substances including pesticides, heavy metals, and industrial chemicals. Pesticides and herbicides, used in agricultural practices, can leach into groundwater and surface water, introducing harmful chemicals such as atrazine, glyphosate, and other endocrine disruptors into the water supply. Heavy metals like lead, arsenic, and mercury can enter water through industrial processes, aging infrastructure, and natural mineral deposits. These chemicals are insidious, as they may not alter the taste or appearance of water, yet prolonged exposure can lead to serious health issues including neurological damage, reproductive problems, and an increased risk of cancer. Utilizing activated carbon filters or reverse osmosis systems can effectively reduce chemical contaminants in water.

Physical contaminants primarily affect the aesthetic qualities of water, including its appearance, taste, and odor, but can also pose health risks. Sediment, organic material, and other particulates can carry with them a host of chemical and biological contaminants, while also making water unpalatable. Filtration methods that include mechanical filters to remove sediments, coupled with carbon filters for taste and odor improvement, are effective in addressing physical contaminants.

The health risks associated with contaminated water cannot be overstated. Biological contaminants can lead to acute sickness, debilitating diseases, and even death, particularly in vulnerable populations such as children, the elderly, and those with compromised immune systems. Chemical contaminants, on the other hand, may have more insidious effects, with symptoms and diseases developing over years of exposure. Physical contaminants, while often less directly harmful, can indicate the presence of or carry more dangerous biological or chemical contaminants.

In preparing for and managing water purification in a survival scenario, understanding these contaminants and their sources is the first step. Implementing a multi-barrier approach to water treatment that includes filtration, disinfection, and possibly chemical treatment is essential for ensuring the safety of your water supply. Regular testing of water sources, when possible, can also provide valuable information on the presence and levels of various contaminants, guiding treatment decisions and ensuring the health and well-being of all who rely on the water.

Boiling and Filtration Methods

Boiling water is one of the most effective methods to kill pathogens including bacteria, viruses, and protozoa that can cause diseases. To ensure the water reaches a temperature where all pathogens are killed, it should be brought to a rolling boil. A rolling boil is when the water is bubbling vigorously, producing steam. This state should be maintained for at least one minute at sea level. For those living at altitudes above 5,000 feet, the boiling time should be extended to three minutes due to the decrease in boiling temperature at higher elevations. It's crucial to start timing only after the water has reached a full rolling boil. Using a lid on the pot can help achieve a boil faster and conserve fuel. After boiling, let the water cool naturally without adding ice or cold water, as this could reintroduce contaminants.

For additional safety, water should be filtered before boiling to remove any physical particles. Basic filtration can be achieved using a clean cloth, coffee filter, or paper towel placed over the mouth of a container to catch sediment, debris, and other visible contaminants as the water is poured through. This pre-filtration process enhances the effectiveness of boiling by removing substances that could shelter microorganisms from the heat.

For a more thorough filtration that can address smaller particulates and improve the taste, odor, and color of water, a DIY sand and charcoal filter can be constructed. Begin by cutting the bottom off a large plastic bottle or using a PVC pipe section. Layer clean sand, activated charcoal, and gravel inside, starting with gravel at the bottom followed by charcoal then sand at the top. This setup mimics natural filtration processes and can help reduce the presence of some chemical contaminants. Water should be passed through this filter slowly to maximize contact time with the charcoal, which is effective at adsorbing chemicals and some heavy metals. It's important to note, however, that while this method can significantly improve water quality, it does not eliminate all pathogens or chemical contaminants, making boiling or chemical disinfection necessary for ensuring water safety.

Activated charcoal can be sourced from aquarium supplies or created by charring wood or coconut shells at high temperatures in the absence of oxygen. The charcoal should be crushed and rinsed to remove any dust before use in filtration. Regular replacement of the charcoal and sand is necessary to maintain the efficacy of the filter, with the frequency depending on the volume of water filtered and the level of contaminants.

These simple yet effective methods for water purification can be lifesaving in emergency situations where access to clean water is compromised. By understanding and applying these techniques, individuals can ensure a safer water supply for themselves and their families during crises.

Advanced Water Purification Systems

In the realm of ensuring a safe drinking water supply during prolonged emergencies or off-grid living scenarios, advanced water purification systems stand as a critical line of defense against a wide array of contaminants that simpler boiling and basic filtration methods might not address. Among these advanced options, reverse osmosis systems and ultraviolet (UV) purifiers represent two of the most effective technologies available for home use, each with its unique mechanism for purifying water.

Reverse osmosis (RO) systems utilize a semi-permeable membrane to remove ions, unwanted molecules, and larger particles from drinking water. In an RO system, water is forced under pressure through the membrane, leaving contaminants behind, which are then flushed away. This process is highly effective at reducing a broad spectrum of contaminants, including dissolved salts, bacteria, and viruses. For optimal performance, an RO system should be equipped with a pre-filter to remove sediment and a post-filter to catch any residual contaminants post-RO process. It's important to note that RO systems require a considerable amount of water to produce a small amount of purified water, a factor known as wastewater ratio, and they may also remove beneficial minerals from the water, which might necessitate re-mineralization steps.

UV purifiers, on the other hand, employ ultraviolet light to disinfect water by damaging the DNA and RNA of bacteria, viruses, and other pathogens, rendering them incapable of reproducing and causing illness. This method of purification is highly effective against microorganisms and is advantageous because it does not introduce chemicals into the water. However, UV purifiers require clear water to function effectively, as turbidity can shield pathogens from UV light exposure. Therefore, pre-filtration to remove sediment and particulates is often necessary. Additionally, UV purifiers depend on electricity or batteries to power the UV lamp, which could be a limitation in some emergency scenarios.

Portable water purifiers and treatment tablets offer a more mobile solution for water purification, catering to the needs of individuals who might need to purify water away from their home base. Portable purifiers often combine several purification methods, such as carbon filtration coupled with mechanical filtration and, in some cases, UV light treatment. These devices are designed for ease of use, allowing for the purification of water from virtually any source while on the move. However, their capacity is generally limited, making them more suitable for individual or small-group use rather than as a solution for household water needs.

Water purification tablets, containing substances like iodine or chlorine dioxide, offer a lightweight and compact option for disinfecting water. These tablets are effective against many pathogens but may leave an aftertaste and are not effective against all types of contaminants, such as chemical pollutants. Furthermore, there's a waiting period from the time the tablet is added to the water until it's safe to drink, which can vary depending on the product.

When selecting an advanced water purification system, it's crucial to consider the specific needs of your household, including the types of contaminants present in your water source, the volume of water you need to purify, and whether portability is a requirement. Regular maintenance is also key to ensuring these systems continue to operate effectively, including membrane replacement for RO systems, bulb replacement for UV purifiers, and periodic testing of water quality to verify the removal of contaminants. By integrating these advanced purification methods into your overall water security strategy, you can significantly enhance your resilience in the face of water-related challenges, ensuring a reliable supply of safe drinking water for your family under a wide range of conditions.

Building a DIY Water Purification System

Materials
- 2 five-gallon buckets with lids

- Ceramic water filter with a spigot
- Drill with 1/2 inch and 1/4 inch drill bits
- Two rubber O-rings
- One rubber washer
- One wingnut that fits the ceramic filter's threaded end
- Non-toxic silicone sealant
- Activated charcoal
- Coarse sand
- Fine sand
- Gravel
- Clean cloth or coffee filter
- Plastic tubing (optional for extension)

Tools
- Drill
- Measuring tape
- Sharpie or marker for marking drill points
- Wrench or pliers for tightening the wingnut

Step-by-step instructions

1. **Prepare the Buckets:** Drill a 1/2 inch hole at the bottom of one bucket. This will be the top bucket where the filtration happens. Drill a 1/4 inch hole in the lid of the other bucket; this will be the bottom bucket where the filtered water is collected.

2. **Assemble the Filter:** Insert the ceramic filter's spout through the 1/2 inch hole in the bottom of the top bucket. Secure it with a rubber washer on the inside and tighten with a wingnut. Ensure a tight fit to prevent leaks. Optionally, apply non-toxic silicone sealant around the edges for an extra seal.

3. **Create the Filtration Layers:** Place a clean cloth or coffee filter at the bottom of the top bucket, over the hole, to prevent sand from entering the ceramic filter. Add 2 inches of fine sand, followed by 2 inches of coarse sand, and then 2-3 inches of gravel. Each layer should be leveled and compacted slightly.

4. **Add Activated Charcoal:** Spread a layer of activated charcoal about 1 inch thick on top of the gravel. This will help remove chemicals and improve the taste of the water.

5. **Final Assembly:** Place the top bucket (with the filtration materials and ceramic filter) on the lid of the bottom bucket. Ensure the ceramic filter's spigot aligns with the hole in the lid of the bottom bucket.

6. **Begin Filtering:** Pour water into the top bucket and allow it to slowly filter through to the bottom bucket. The first few gallons should be discarded as they are used to prime the filter and wash away any loose particles from the materials.

7. **Collecting Water:** Once the water starts collecting in the bottom bucket, use the spigot attached to the ceramic filter to access the purified water.

Safety tips

- Ensure all materials, especially the buckets and sand, are clean and free from contaminants before assembling the filter.
- When drilling holes in the buckets, wear safety goggles to protect your eyes from plastic shavings.
- Wash your hands thoroughly before handling the filtration materials to avoid introducing contaminants.

Maintenance

- The ceramic filter should be cleaned periodically according to the manufacturer's instructions, usually by scrubbing the surface with a brush under running water.
- Replace the activated charcoal every 2-3 months, or after filtering approximately 100 gallons of water, to ensure effectiveness.
- The sand and gravel layers should be replaced yearly to maintain filtration quality.

Difficulty rating ★★☆☆☆

Variations

- For larger volumes of water, a third bucket can be added to the system. Drill matching holes in the bottom of the second and top of the third bucket, stacking them. This allows for additional filtration stages or increased storage capacity.
- If cleaner water sources are scarce, pre-filter water through a cloth or sieve to remove large debris before it enters the DIY filtration system to prolong the life of the filter materials.

Video BONUS

Chapter 6: Off-Grid Energy Solutions

Powering Your Home Off-Grid

Assessing Your Energy Needs

Preparation

1. Gather previous utility bills for reference.
2. List all electrical appliances and systems in your home.
3. Have a notebook or spreadsheet ready for calculations.

Materials

- Utility bills from the past 12 months
- Notebook or digital spreadsheet
- Calculator
- Energy use monitor or watt-meter (optional for precise appliance measurements)

Tools

- Pen or pencil
- Computer with spreadsheet software (optional)

Step-by-step instructions

1. **Collect Utility Bills:** Start by gathering your utility bills for the last year to get an average monthly energy consumption. This will give you a baseline of your total energy usage.

2. **List Appliances and Systems:** Make a comprehensive list of all electrical appliances, lighting, and systems in your home. Include everything from large appliances like refrigerators and HVAC systems to smaller items like laptops and phone chargers.

3. **Estimate Usage:** For each item on your list, estimate how many hours per day it's used. If you're unsure, a quick internet search can provide average usage times for common appliances.

4. **Calculate Wattage:** Check the wattage of each appliance (usually found on the appliance itself or in the manual). If actual wattage is not known, use a standard wattage list for common household items.

5. **Compute Daily Energy Consumption:** Multiply the wattage by the number of hours used per day for each appliance. This will give you the daily energy consumption in watt-hours (Wh) for each item.

6. **Summarize Monthly Consumption:** Add up the daily energy consumption of all items to find your total daily consumption. Multiply this by 30 to estimate your monthly energy needs in watt-hours.

7. **Prioritize Essential Needs:** Identify which appliances and systems are absolutely necessary during an emergency (e.g., refrigerator, lights, HVAC, medical devices). This will help you prioritize energy needs.

8. **Consider Reduction Strategies:** Look for opportunities to reduce energy consumption, such as switching to LED bulbs, unplugging idle electronics, or using energy-efficient appliances.

9. **Calculate Off-Grid System Requirements:** Based on your prioritized list of essential needs, calculate the total watt-hours required per day. Add a 20% buffer to this number to account for inefficiencies and unforeseen energy needs.

10. **Plan for Energy Production and Storage:** Use your total daily watt-hour requirement to determine the size of the off-grid energy system needed, including solar panels, wind turbines, batteries, and/or generators.

Safety tips

- When using a watt-meter or energy use monitor, ensure that you follow the manufacturer's instructions to avoid electrical hazards.
- Always unplug an appliance before attempting to inspect its wattage rating physically.

Maintenance

- Regularly review and update your energy needs assessment, especially if you add new appliances or if your lifestyle changes significantly.
- Check the condition and efficiency of your essential appliances periodically, as older units may consume more power than newer, more efficient models.

Difficulty rating ★★☆☆☆

Variations

- For those with fluctuating energy needs or seasonal variations, consider performing this assessment at different times of the year to account for changes in heating, cooling, and lighting requirements.
- Advanced users may wish to install energy use monitors on major appliances for real-time tracking and more accurate data over time.

Designing an Off-Grid Energy System

Designing an off-grid energy system requires a comprehensive understanding of the components that make up a robust and reliable setup capable of meeting your home's energy needs without reliance on the traditional power grid. At the core of an off-grid system are generators, batteries, and solar panels, each playing a pivotal role in energy production, storage, and supply. The integration of these components not only ensures a continuous power supply but also enhances the system's resilience to outages and environmental variables.

Starting with solar panels, the cornerstone of harnessing renewable energy, it's imperative to select panels with a high efficiency rate to maximize electricity generation even on days with limited sunlight. Opt for monocrystalline solar panels known for their superior performance and longevity. Placement is equally critical; panels should be installed in a location that receives maximum direct sunlight exposure throughout the day, ideally on a south-facing roof or ground mount system free from shade. The tilt angle of the panels should be adjusted according to your geographical location to optimize the angle of incidence between the solar panels and the sun's rays, enhancing energy capture.

Batteries play a crucial role in storing the energy generated by solar panels for use during nighttime or overcast days. Lithium-ion batteries are recommended due to their high energy density, longer lifespan, and ability to maintain consistent power output. The capacity of your battery bank should be sized based on your household's average energy consumption and the autonomy desired, typically calculated by evaluating your home's energy needs during the least sunny periods of the year. It's essential to incorporate a battery management system (BMS) to monitor battery health, manage charge and discharge cycles, and ensure the longevity of your storage system.

Generators, while not a primary energy source in an eco-conscious off-grid setup, serve as a critical backup during prolonged periods of insufficient sunlight or unusually high energy demands. A dual-fuel generator capable of running on propane or gasoline offers flexibility and reliability. The generator should be integrated into the system with an automatic transfer switch that activates the generator when battery levels drop below a predefined threshold, ensuring an uninterrupted power supply.

The integration of these components necessitates a sophisticated yet user-friendly energy management system (EMS) capable of optimizing the flow of electricity from generation to storage and finally to consumption. The EMS should intelligently switch between energy sources based on availability and demand, prioritize solar energy use, manage battery charging and discharging, and start the backup generator when necessary, all while providing real-time monitoring and control over your energy system.

Incorporating additional renewable energy sources, such as wind turbines, can further enhance the system's reliability and reduce dependency on the backup generator. Small-scale wind turbines complement solar panels effectively, especially in areas with higher wind speeds during the night or winter months when solar production may decrease.

The design of your off-grid energy system should also include safety components such as circuit breakers, surge protectors, and disconnect switches to protect against electrical hazards and ensure the system's safe operation. Proper grounding and lightning protection are paramount, especially for outdoor components like solar panels and wind turbines.

In conclusion, designing an off-grid energy system requires careful consideration of each component's selection and integration to create a seamless, efficient, and reliable power solution tailored to your specific energy needs and environmental conditions. By meticulously planning your system, you can achieve energy independence, reduce your carbon footprint, and ensure a stable power supply for your home regardless of external power grid conditions.

Backup Power Sources

Ensuring a continuous power supply during extended outages necessitates a comprehensive approach to backup power sources, focusing on batteries and energy storage solutions as critical components of an off-grid energy system. The resilience of your home's power supply in the face of prolonged grid failures or natural disasters hinges on the strategic selection and management of these backup options.

Batteries, particularly lithium-ion types, stand at the forefront of energy storage solutions due to their high energy density, efficiency, and longer cycle life compared to traditional lead-acid batteries. When configuring a battery bank for your off-grid system, it's imperative to calculate your household's energy consumption meticulously. This involves tallying up the wattage of essential appliances and systems that need to remain operational during an outage and determining the total energy consumed over a 24-hour period. With this data in hand, aim to have a battery capacity that can sustain your critical load for at least three to five days without recharging. This buffer allows for periods of low sunlight or other renewable energy generation shortfalls.

The integration of a Battery Management System (BMS) is non-negotiable for safeguarding your battery bank. A BMS monitors the voltage, temperature, and state of charge of each battery cell, preventing overcharging, deep discharging, and overheating, thus extending the lifespan of the battery bank. For added redundancy, consider configuring your battery bank in a modular setup. This way, if one segment of the bank fails, the system can continue to operate on the remaining segments, ensuring an uninterrupted power supply.

Beyond batteries, diversifying your backup power sources enhances system reliability. Dual-fuel generators, capable of operating on propane or gasoline, offer a versatile and immediate source of power when renewable energy sources fall short. The automatic transfer switch is a critical component, seamlessly transitioning your power supply from the battery bank to the generator when battery levels dip below a set threshold. This automation ensures that your home remains powered without manual intervention, crucial during the night or when away from home.

For those seeking to minimize reliance on fossil fuels, incorporating a secondary renewable energy source, such as a wind turbine, can complement solar panels effectively. Wind energy can be particularly valuable during winter months or at night when solar production is minimal. The energy generated by the wind turbine can either be directly used to power your home or diverted to recharge the battery bank, providing a continuous cycle of energy production and storage.

Maintenance plays a pivotal role in the reliability of backup power sources. Regular checks and servicing of generators, cleaning of solar panels and wind turbines, and inspection of battery terminals and connections ensure optimal performance and prevent system failures. Additionally, staying informed about advancements in battery technology and energy storage solutions can lead to system upgrades that increase storage capacity, efficiency, and sustainability.

By meticulously planning and managing your home's backup power sources, you create a robust off-grid energy system capable of sustaining your household through extended power outages. This strategic approach not only secures your energy independence but also ensures the safety and comfort of your loved ones in times of crisis, embodying the essence of preparedness and resilience.

Exploring Solar, Wind, Generator Options

Solar Power Systems

Materials
- Monocrystalline solar panels, suitable for high-efficiency needs in limited space
- Polycrystalline solar panels for a cost-effective solution with slightly lower efficiency
- Mounting hardware including brackets and bolts, specifically designed for solar panel installation
- Charge controller, preferably MPPT (Maximum Power Point Tracking) for optimal energy conversion
- Deep cycle batteries, such as AGM (Absorbent Glass Mat) or Lithium-ion, for energy storage
- Inverter to convert DC (Direct Current) from the panels/batteries to AC (Alternating Current) for home use
- MC4 connectors for secure electrical connections between panels

- Electrical wiring, UV and weather-resistant, for outdoor applications
- Grounding equipment to protect the system from lightning strikes and electrical surges
- Cable management tools like conduit, cable ties, and wire clips for a neat installation

Tools
- Drill with various size bits for mounting brackets and hardware
- Wire strippers and crimpers specifically for MC4 connectors
- Wrench set for tightening bolts and nuts in the mounting hardware
- Multimeter for electrical testing and troubleshooting
- Safety glasses and gloves to protect against potential hazards
- Ladder for accessing roof or installation site
- Solar panel tilt meter to determine the optimal angle for installation
- Level to ensure panels are installed at the correct angle for maximum sunlight exposure

Step-by-step instructions

1. **Site Assessment:** Choose an area with maximum direct sunlight exposure, ideally south-facing, with minimal shading from trees or structures during the day. Use a solar pathfinder or app to analyze sun exposure throughout the year.
2. **Determine System Size:** Calculate your daily energy usage in kilowatt-hours (kWh) and design your solar system size accordingly. Factor in your region's peak sunlight hours to estimate the total wattage needed from your solar panels.
3. **Select Solar Panel Type:** Based on your energy needs and available space, choose between monocrystalline or polycrystalline panels. Monocrystalline panels are more efficient but costlier, while polycrystalline panels offer a good balance between cost and efficiency.
4. **Mounting System Installation:** Install the mounting hardware according to the manufacturer's instructions, ensuring it's securely fastened to roof rafters or a stable ground frame. Use a level to ensure the mounts are evenly placed.
5. **Panel Installation:** Attach the solar panels to the mounting system, securing them with the provided brackets and bolts. Ensure there's a slight tilt towards the south (in the Northern Hemisphere) to maximize sun exposure.
6. **Wiring:** Connect the solar panels in series or parallel, depending on your system voltage and amperage requirements. Use MC4 connectors for secure and weatherproof connections. Route the cables to the charge controller location, using conduit for protection.
7. **Install Charge Controller and Inverter:** Connect the solar panel wires to the charge controller, then connect the charge controller to the batteries. Install the inverter close to the batteries, connecting it to both the battery bank and your home's electrical panel.

8. **Battery Bank Setup:** If using a battery system for energy storage, connect your batteries in series or parallel to match the system's voltage and capacity requirements. Ensure proper ventilation for batteries that emit gases.

9. **System Grounding:** Ground the solar panel system to protect against electrical surges and lightning strikes. Install grounding rods and connect them to the system's frame and components as per local electrical codes.

10. **Final Testing:** Use a multimeter to test the voltage and current output from the panels to ensure they match the expected values. Check all connections for tightness and proper installation.

Safety tips

- Always wear safety glasses and gloves when handling solar panels and electrical components.
- Ensure the main electrical supply to your home is turned off when connecting the solar system to your home's electrical panel.
- Follow all local codes and regulations for electrical and building standards.

Maintenance

- Regularly clean the solar panels with water and a soft brush to remove dust and debris that could reduce efficiency.
- Check the system's connections and mounting hardware annually for signs of wear or damage.
- Monitor the system's energy output to identify any potential issues or drops in performance.

Difficulty rating ★★★☆☆

Variations

- For homes with limited space, consider installing adjustable tilt mounts to optimize the angle of your panels seasonally.
- In areas with frequent power outages, include a backup generator as part of your off-grid system for additional reliability.

Wind Power for Home Defense

Harnessing wind energy for home use presents a sustainable and efficient off-grid power solution, tapping into the natural and renewable resource of wind to generate electricity. Wind turbines convert kinetic energy from wind into mechanical power, which a generator then converts into electricity usable in homes. This process involves the movement of air turning the turbine's blades, which spins a shaft connected to a generator. The effectiveness of wind turbines in generating sufficient power hinges on several factors, including wind speed, turbine size, and the efficiency of the generator.

To assess the suitability of wind power for a specific location, one must first understand the average wind speeds in the area. Areas with average wind speeds of at least 10 miles per hour are generally considered suitable for wind turbine operation. It's crucial to analyze wind speed data over different seasons to ensure consistent energy production throughout the year. The installation site should be free of obstructions that could block or divert wind flow, such as tall buildings or dense forests. Ideally, the turbine should be mounted on a tower, positioned at least 30 feet above any obstacle within a 300-foot radius to maximize wind exposure.

Choosing the right wind turbine involves considering the energy needs of your household and the wind conditions of your location. For residential use, turbines range from small 400-watt models, suitable for supplementing existing power sources, to 15-kilowatt systems capable of fully powering a home. The rotor diameter of the turbine directly impacts its energy production capabilities; larger blades can capture more wind. However, the size of the system should be balanced with the available space and local zoning regulations, which may restrict the height or location of the turbine.

Installation of a wind turbine requires careful planning and adherence to local building codes and permits. It's advisable to consult with professionals who can conduct a detailed site assessment, recommend the appropriate system size, and ensure the installation meets all legal and safety standards. Additionally, integrating the wind power system with your home's existing electrical grid and possibly a battery storage system will require expert guidance to optimize energy use and storage.

Maintenance is another critical aspect of utilizing wind power. Regular inspections and upkeep of the turbine, tower, and electrical components are necessary to ensure long-term reliability and performance. This includes checking for wear and tear on the blades, ensuring bolts are tightened, and verifying the integrity of electrical connections.

In conclusion, wind power offers a viable and environmentally friendly option for off-grid energy solutions, particularly in areas with favorable wind conditions. By thoroughly assessing your location's wind resources, choosing the right turbine for your needs, and adhering to maintenance best practices, you can harness the power of the wind to sustainably meet your household's energy needs without a detailed summary or closing remarks to encapsulate the discussed points.

Generator Backup Power and Safety

Generators serve as a critical backup power source, ensuring that your home remains operational during outages or off-grid living situations. Understanding the different types of generators and their specific uses can help you select the right one for your needs, ensuring that you can maintain power to essential systems and devices when the grid is down. Portable generators are versatile and can be moved as needed, making them ideal for temporary power needs or smaller applications such as powering a few appliances or tools. They typically run on gasoline, diesel, or propane, offering flexibility in fuel choice based on availability and preference. Standby generators, on the other hand, are permanently installed outside the home and automatically activate in the event of a power outage. These systems are connected directly to your home's electrical panel and fueled by an existing natural gas or propane line, providing a seamless transition to backup power without manual intervention. Dual-fuel generators offer the ability to switch between two types of fuel, usually gasoline and propane, providing an added layer of versatility and reliability in situations where one fuel type may be more readily available than the other.

When selecting a generator, consider the wattage requirements of the appliances and systems you need to power. Calculate the total wattage by adding up the starting watts (the initial surge required to start the motor) and running watts (the continuous power required to operate the appliance) of each device. This will help you determine the generator size you need to meet your power demands. Safety considerations are paramount when operating generators. Always place portable generators outdoors and away from windows, doors, and vents to prevent carbon monoxide poisoning. Ensure the generator is placed on a stable, level surface to reduce the risk of tipping and spillage. Standby generators should be professionally installed by a licensed electrician to ensure they comply with local building codes and safety standards. Regular maintenance is crucial for the reliability of your generator. For portable models, this includes checking oil levels, cleaning or replacing air filters, and running the generator periodically to ensure it's ready for use. Standby generators typically have self-testing features but should still be inspected annually by a professional to check fuel lines, battery health, and overall system functionality.

Properly integrating a generator into your home's energy system requires careful planning and adherence to safety protocols. For portable generators, use heavy-duty, outdoor-rated extension cords to connect appliances directly to the generator, or have a transfer switch installed by a professional to safely power hardwired systems without the risk of backfeeding the electrical grid. Standby generators automatically disconnect from the grid when they activate, providing a safe and efficient transition to backup power.

In summary, generators are a vital component of a comprehensive off-grid energy solution, providing reliable backup power to keep your home running during outages. By understanding the types of generators available, their fuel requirements, and the importance of safety and maintenance, you can ensure a dependable power source that enhances your home's resilience and security.

Energy Conservation Strategies

Reducing Energy Consumption at Home

Reducing energy consumption within the home not only contributes to a more sustainable planet but also significantly lowers monthly utility bills, making it a crucial aspect of off-grid living and emergency preparedness. The first step towards minimizing daily energy use is conducting an energy audit to identify where the most power is being consumed and where you can make the most impactful changes. Look for outdated appliances that can be replaced with **Energy Star-rated** models, which use 10 to 50 percent less energy and water than standard models. Replacing an old refrigerator, for example, with a newer, energy-efficient model can save up to $300 a year in energy costs.

One of the simplest yet effective strategies to reduce power needs is to switch to **LED lighting**. LEDs use at least 75 percent less energy and last 25 times longer than incandescent lighting. Consider installing motion sensors or timers on outdoor lights to ensure they are only on when needed, further reducing unnecessary power consumption.

Another critical area is heating and cooling, which accounts for a large portion of home energy use. Proper insulation and sealing of windows and doors can prevent heat loss during winter and keep cool air inside during summer. Installing a programmable thermostat can save up to 10 percent a year on heating and cooling by automatically lowering or raising the temperature during sleeping or away times. For those living in climates that require significant heating, consider a **pellet stove** as a more efficient alternative to traditional wood stoves or electric heaters. Pellet stoves burn compressed wood or biomass pellets, making them cleaner and more cost-effective.

Water heating is another significant energy consumer. Lowering the water heater temperature to 120 degrees Fahrenheit can reduce heating costs by 6 to 10 percent. Investing in a **tankless water heater** that heats water on demand instead of maintaining a tank of hot water 24/7 can lead to even greater savings.

For those looking to make substantial reductions in their energy consumption, **solar panels** offer a way to harness renewable energy directly from the sun. Modern solar installations can be scaled to meet almost any power need, from powering a single appliance to running an entire home. Additionally, the cost of solar panels has decreased dramatically over the past decade, making it an increasingly viable option for homeowners. Pairing a solar array with a **battery storage system** allows for energy to be stored during peak production times for use during the night or on cloudy days, ensuring a consistent and reliable power supply.

Incorporating these strategies into your home not only prepares you for off-grid living or emergencies but also moves you towards a more sustainable lifestyle. By focusing on energy-efficient appliances, lighting solutions, and renewable energy sources, you can significantly reduce your daily energy consumption, save money, and contribute to a healthier environment for future generations.

Seasonal Energy Conservation Tips

Adapting your energy usage according to seasonal changes is essential for maintaining an efficient and sustainable off-grid living situation. As the seasons shift, so do the demands on your home's energy system. In the warmer months, the focus is on keeping your home cool without overburdening your energy reserves, while in the colder months, the challenge lies in heating your home efficiently. Understanding how to modify your energy usage with the changing seasons not only conserves energy but also ensures your off-grid system can support your needs year-round.

During the summer, maximizing natural ventilation can significantly reduce the need for powered cooling systems. Design your living spaces to encourage cross-ventilation; open windows on opposite sides of the home to allow air to flow freely, cooling your space naturally. Consider installing reflective window coatings or using thermal drapes to block out heat from direct sunlight, reducing the greenhouse effect inside your home. Solar-powered attic fans can expel hot air from the highest points in your home, preventing it from becoming a heat reservoir that makes cooling more challenging.

In contrast, winter demands a strategy focused on retaining heat and minimizing energy loss. Start by ensuring your home is well-insulated; this includes walls, floors, and especially the attic, where heat can easily escape. Use weather stripping around doors and windows to seal any gaps that might allow cold air in and warm air out. Investing in thermal curtains can also help by adding an extra layer of insulation to windows, a common point of heat loss. On sunny days, open curtains on south-facing windows to allow natural sunlight to warm your interior spaces, then close them as the sun sets to retain the heat.

Transitioning into spring and fall, the emphasis shifts to preparing your home for the more extreme temperatures to come. These seasons are ideal for performing maintenance on your energy systems, including cleaning solar panels, servicing your wind turbine, and ensuring all battery connections are secure and corrosion-free. It's also a perfect time to reassess your home's insulation and seal any leaks discovered during the more extreme weather months.

Heating and cooling strategies for off-grid living must also consider the use of energy-efficient appliances and systems. A wood stove or pellet stove can be an effective way to heat your home in the winter, using renewable resources that you may be able to source from your own property. For cooling, evaporative coolers can offer a low-energy alternative to traditional air conditioners in dry climates, using the natural process of water evaporation to cool the air.

Finally, regardless of the season, LED lighting should be used throughout your home to reduce energy consumption. LEDs are not only more energy-efficient than traditional bulbs but also emit less heat, which is particularly beneficial during the summer months.

By implementing these seasonal energy conservation tips, you can significantly reduce your energy consumption, ensuring your off-grid living situation remains sustainable and comfortable throughout the year. Each season brings its own set of challenges and opportunities for energy conservation, and by planning ahead and making thoughtful adjustments to your energy use, you can maintain an efficient and sustainable home no matter the weather outside.

Smart Energy Management Systems

In the realm of off-grid living and energy conservation, **Smart Energy Management Systems (SEMS)** stand out as a pivotal technology, enabling homeowners to optimize energy use and significantly reduce wastage. These systems integrate seamlessly with various energy sources and appliances within your home, providing real-time data and control over your energy consumption. By utilizing SEMS, you can monitor and manage the energy generated from solar panels, wind turbines, and other renewable sources, ensuring that every watt is used efficiently.

A core component of SEMS is the **energy management controller**, a sophisticated device that acts as the brain of your home's energy system. It gathers data from sensors placed throughout your home and energy-generating systems, analyzing patterns in energy consumption and production. This controller can automatically adjust settings on appliances, heating and cooling systems, and lighting based on your preferences and the most efficient use of available energy. For instance, it might lower the thermostat during peak solar production hours to cool the house, taking advantage of the surplus energy without drawing from the grid or stored power.

To effectively implement a SEMS, it's crucial to equip your home with **smart appliances** and devices that can communicate with the management controller. These might include smart thermostats, which adjust the indoor temperature based on your daily schedule and weather forecasts; smart lighting systems that dim or turn off lights in unoccupied rooms; and smart plugs that can cut power to devices in standby mode, reducing phantom load. Each of these devices contributes to a holistic approach to energy management, where no energy is wasted, and all consumption is intentional and optimized.

Another significant advantage of SEMS is the ability to **store and distribute energy** on demand. By integrating with battery storage systems, SEMS can decide the best times to store energy or draw from it based on peak demand charges, weather predictions, and your personal schedule. For example, it can charge the battery system during low-demand periods or when renewable energy production is high, then use this stored energy during peak hours or when production is low, thus avoiding expensive grid energy use.

User interfaces play a vital role in the effectiveness of SEMS. Modern systems come with intuitive apps and dashboards that allow homeowners to monitor their energy consumption and production in real-time. These interfaces display detailed analytics on energy use trends, potential savings, and even environmental impact. They empower users to make informed decisions about their energy habits, encouraging a more sustainable lifestyle. For instance, you might notice that energy consumption spikes during certain times of the day and adjust your usage or settings accordingly.

For those looking to implement SEMS, starting with a comprehensive **energy audit** of your home is advisable. This will identify the most significant energy drains and opportunities for improvement. Following this, investing in compatible smart devices and an energy management controller tailored to your specific needs and energy goals is essential. Professional installation and setup are recommended to ensure that all components of the SEMS are correctly integrated and configured for optimal performance.

Incorporating SEMS into your off-grid energy solution not only enhances your ability to manage energy more effectively but also aligns with broader objectives of reducing carbon footprint, saving on energy costs, and promoting a sustainable, self-sufficient lifestyle. As technology advances, the capabilities of these systems will only grow, offering even greater control and efficiency in home energy management.

Video BONUS

Chapter 7: Medical Preparedness

Building a Home First Aid Kit

Basic First Aid Kit Components

In building a comprehensive home first aid kit, the foundation lies in assembling a core set of supplies that address a wide range of emergencies, from minor cuts and abrasions to more serious injuries requiring immediate response before professional medical help can be obtained. The essentials of emergency first aid include a variety of gauze pads in multiple sizes to cover and protect wounds, ensuring that they are sterile to prevent infection. Bandages, both adhesive and non-adhesive types, play a crucial role in securing gauze pads in place, supporting injured limbs, and applying pressure to stop bleeding. It's advisable to have a range of bandages, including elastic wraps for sprains and strains, as well as butterfly bandages for deeper cuts that may need temporary closure.

Antiseptics are indispensable in a first aid kit for cleaning wounds and preventing infections. Items such as isopropyl alcohol, hydrogen peroxide, and antiseptic wipes should be included, alongside antibiotic ointment to apply on cuts and scrapes after they've been cleaned. It's important to use these products according to their instructions to avoid any adverse reactions, especially in individuals with sensitive skin or allergies.

Wound care essentials extend to include tools that facilitate the cleaning and dressing of injuries. Scissors with blunt ends are necessary for cutting bandages and tape to the required sizes without causing additional injury. Tweezers are invaluable for removing debris such as glass, splinters, or dirt from wounds before dressing them. A digital thermometer is a must-have for monitoring body temperature, especially in situations where infection might be a concern. It's beneficial to have a thermometer that provides quick readings and is easy to clean for repeated use.

Furthermore, the first aid kit should contain a variety of adhesive tape to secure bandages and dressings, sterile cotton balls and swabs for applying antiseptics, and disposable gloves to maintain hygiene and prevent the spread of infection while treating wounds. Pain relievers, such as acetaminophen or ibuprofen, can be included to manage discomfort or fever, but it's crucial to be aware of any potential allergies or contraindications in family members.

Each item in the first aid kit serves a specific purpose, and together, they form a comprehensive response to a variety of medical emergencies that might occur at home. Ensuring that these supplies are well-organized, easily accessible, and regularly checked for expiration dates and replenishment needs will enhance your preparedness for effectively handling common injuries and health issues, thereby safeguarding the well-being of your loved ones until professional medical care can be sought if necessary.

Advanced Medical Supplies

In the realm of preparedness, especially when fortifying your home against potential crises, the inclusion of advanced medical supplies can significantly elevate your ability to respond effectively to emergencies. Beyond the basics covered in your first aid kit, certain situations may necessitate a more sophisticated approach to injury management. This is where items such as **suture kits**, **splints**, **emergency tourniquets**, specialized **burn treatments, eye wash solutions**, and **specialized dressings** come into play, each serving a unique and critical role in your medical preparedness arsenal.

Suture kits are indispensable for closing deep cuts or lacerations that cannot be adequately treated with adhesive strips or bandages alone. A comprehensive kit should include sterile needles, suture thread, and scissors, complemented by antiseptic wipes or solutions to ensure a clean working area. Familiarizing yourself with basic suturing techniques through courses or guided tutorials can be invaluable, as this skill can prevent infections and promote better healing outcomes.

Splints serve the essential function of immobilizing broken or fractured bones, reducing pain, and preventing further injury. Materials for splinting can range from rigid items like boards or metal strips to more flexible options such as padded aluminum splints that can be molded to the shape of the limb. Including a variety of sizes and materials ensures you can effectively stabilize different parts of the body as needed.

Emergency tourniquets are critical for controlling severe bleeding that bandages cannot manage. A properly applied tourniquet can be lifesaving, especially in situations where medical help is delayed. Opt for commercially made tourniquets that offer reliability and ease of use, and educate yourself on their correct application to avoid causing additional harm.

For **burn treatments**, stock a range of supplies that address both the immediate pain relief and the longer-term healing process. This includes hydrogel-based burn dressings, which cool the burn and provide a protective barrier against infection, and burn creams or sprays that contain aloe vera or other soothing agents. It's also wise to have sterile gauze and bandages specifically designed for covering burns to keep them clean and protected.

Eye wash solutions are crucial for flushing out irritants, chemicals, or foreign objects that could cause serious damage to the eyes. A portable eye wash station or bottles of sterile saline solution should be readily accessible within your medical kit. Eye injuries can escalate quickly, and having the means to immediately irrigate the eye can prevent long-term vision impairment.

Lastly, **specialized dressings** play a pivotal role in wound care, particularly for injuries that are prone to infection or require a moist healing environment. Options such as hydrocolloid dressings, which promote healing by maintaining a humid condition around the wound, and alginate dressings, ideal for wounds with significant exudate, should be included in your advanced medical supplies.

Each of these advanced medical supplies requires a certain level of knowledge and skill to use effectively. Therefore, it's recommended to seek out training or educational resources that can provide you with the necessary expertise to utilize these tools safely and effectively. Remember, the goal is not just to have these supplies on hand, but to be proficient in their use, ensuring you can provide the best possible care in any situation without hesitation.

Customizing First Aid Kits

Customizing your first aid kit to meet the specific needs of your family is not just prudent; it's essential for ensuring the safety and well-being of each member during emergencies. Every family is unique, with individual health concerns, allergies, and conditions that require special consideration. Therefore, a one-size-fits-all approach to assembling a first aid kit falls short of providing the comprehensive care your loved ones might need in the face of crisis.

For families with **allergies**, it's critical to include antihistamines that can quickly address allergic reactions. Whether it's a reaction to food, insect stings, or environmental allergens, having both oral and topical antihistamines can be life-saving. For severe allergies, an epinephrine auto-injector (EpiPen) should be readily available, and family members must be trained on how to use it correctly.

Chronic conditions such as asthma, diabetes, or heart disease necessitate the inclusion of **prescription medications** in your first aid kit. Asthmatics should have a spare inhaler, while diabetics need an adequate supply of insulin, syringes, or pens, and glucose tablets or gel. For those with heart conditions, ensure that nitroglycerin tablets are within reach. It's also wise to have a detailed list of each family member's medical conditions, medications, dosages, and emergency contacts stored securely within the kit.

When considering the needs of **children**, your kit should include pediatric doses of medications, including pain relievers like acetaminophen or ibuprofen, and a digital thermometer specifically designed for pediatric use. Small bandages, colorful to make the experience less frightening, and child-safe antiseptic wipes can make treating minor injuries less traumatic for young ones. Additionally, incorporating a few small toys or stickers can be a good distraction technique when addressing their injuries.

For **elderly family members**, who may have more fragile skin and a higher risk of falls, your kit should be equipped with larger adhesive bandages, skin protectants, and products designed for sensitive skin. Include a comprehensive list of their current medications and a magnifying glass to help them read labels and dosages accurately. Tools like a pill cutter or crusher can also be invaluable for those who have difficulty swallowing.

Don't forget about **pets**, as they are also family members who may need medical attention. Including pet-specific supplies such as self-cling bandages (which don't stick to fur), styptic powder to stop nail bleeding, and tick removal tools can prepare you for pet-related emergencies. Ensure you have a list of emergency vet contacts and know the basics of pet first aid.

Moreover, for families with unique medical needs, such as those requiring frequent injections or monitoring of conditions, ensure you have a supply of **sterile needles, lancets**, or **test strips**. For conditions that might require immobilization of an injured limb, consider adding a **SAM splint** to your kit, which is versatile and can be molded to fit various needs.

In addition to these specific items, your first aid kit should include **nitrile gloves** to prevent contamination, a **CPR mask** for safe resuscitation efforts, and **saline solution** which can be used for flushing wounds or eyes. A **flashlight** and extra batteries are also essential, especially if you need to address injuries in low-light conditions.

Remember, the goal of customizing your first aid kit is not only to treat injuries but to do so in a manner that is most effective and comforting for the injured person. Regularly review and update your kit to ensure that medications are within their expiration dates and that your supplies remain relevant to your family's evolving needs. By taking these steps, you transform your first aid kit from a collection of supplies into a dynamic resource tailored to protect your family's health and safety.

Essential Medications and Uses

Over-the-Counter Medications

In the realm of medical preparedness, especially within the context of ensuring the safety and well-being of your loved ones in a bug-in scenario, having a well-stocked supply of over-the-counter (OTC) medications is paramount. These OTC essentials serve as the first line of defense against a range of common ailments, from minor injuries and pains to fevers and inflammations, thus playing a critical role in your home pharmacy.

Pain relievers, such as acetaminophen (Tylenol) and ibuprofen (Advil, Motrin), are indispensable in managing pain and reducing fevers. Acetaminophen is recommended for those who need a pain reliever or fever reducer but want to avoid the gastrointestinal side effects associated with NSAIDs (nonsteroidal anti-inflammatory drugs). On the other hand, ibuprofen, an NSAID, is effective in reducing inflammation, pain from injuries, and can also reduce fever. It's crucial to have both options available, as some individuals may have conditions or take medications that contraindicate the use of NSAIDs, making acetaminophen the safer choice.

For those dealing with muscle aches or arthritis, **naproxen sodium** (Aleve) is another NSAID that provides longer-lasting pain relief compared to ibuprofen. However, it's important to monitor its use closely, especially in individuals with cardiovascular risks or kidney issues, due to its potential side effects when used extensively.

Aspirin, while commonly known as a pain reliever, plays a unique role in heart attack prevention for those at risk. In a bug-in situation where access to emergency medical services may be delayed, having aspirin on hand can be a life-saving measure for someone experiencing heart attack symptoms. However, aspirin should not be used for pain relief in children or teenagers due to the risk of Reye's syndrome, a rare but serious condition.

Beyond pain relief, managing fevers is crucial, especially in the context of viral or bacterial infections. Both acetaminophen and ibuprofen are effective in reducing fever, but it's essential to monitor the dosage and frequency to avoid liver damage from acetaminophen or kidney damage from ibuprofen.

For those with allergies, **antihistamines** such as diphenhydramine (Benadryl) and loratadine (Claritin) can provide relief from sneezing, runny nose, and itching. Diphenhydramine, while effective, can cause drowsiness, making loratadine a preferable daytime option for those needing to maintain alertness.

Decongestants like pseudoephedrine (Sudafed) and phenylephrine (found in many combination cold medicines) are effective in relieving nasal congestion but should be used with caution in individuals with high blood pressure.

Antacids and acid reducers such as famotidine (Pepcid) and ranitidine (Zantac) are useful for managing heartburn and indigestion, common issues that can be exacerbated by stress and dietary changes during prolonged indoor stays.

Anti-diarrheal medications, including loperamide (Imodium), are critical for managing symptoms of diarrhea, helping to prevent dehydration and the loss of essential nutrients. In conjunction with oral rehydration solutions, they can be instrumental in managing gastrointestinal disturbances.

Lastly, **first aid ointments** such as triple antibiotic ointments and hydrocortisone cream are essential for treating minor cuts, scrapes, and skin irritations, preventing infection, and promoting healing.

Stocking these OTC medications requires careful consideration of expiration dates and storage conditions to ensure their efficacy when needed. Regularly reviewing and rotating your stock ensures that you are always prepared with effective, safe medications to address common health issues that may arise during a bug-in scenario. Remember, while OTC medications are readily available and effective for many minor conditions, they are not substitutes for professional medical advice or treatment for more serious conditions. Always consult with a healthcare professional for persistent or severe symptoms.

Managing Prescription Medications

Managing and storing prescription medications effectively is a critical component of medical preparedness, especially in scenarios where access to healthcare facilities might be limited. Prescription drugs, vital for managing chronic conditions, require careful handling to maintain their efficacy and ensure they are ready for use when needed. The first step in this process involves creating an inventory of all prescription medications within the household. This inventory should include the name of the medication, the dosage, the prescribing doctor, the pharmacy it was obtained from, and the expiration date. It's crucial to regularly review this inventory, at least every six months, to check for any medications that are nearing their expiration and need replacement.

Storage conditions for prescription medications can significantly affect their potency. Most medications should be stored in a cool, dry place, away from direct sunlight. However, specific storage instructions can vary, with some requiring refrigeration. It's essential to read and follow the storage guidelines provided with each medication. Using original containers with clear labels can help protect the medications from moisture and light while keeping the dosage and expiration date visible. For medications requiring refrigeration, consider investing in a small, dedicated refrigerator or a temperature-controlled storage unit to prevent fluctuations that could compromise the medication's effectiveness.

Another aspect of managing prescription medications is ensuring a sufficient supply. In preparation for emergencies where access to pharmacies might be restricted, aim to have at least a 30-day supply of essential medications on hand. Some insurance policies may limit the amount of medication that can be dispensed at one time, so it's advisable to discuss your needs with your healthcare provider or pharmacist. They may be able to provide a prescription for an extended supply based on emergency preparedness grounds.

For those medications critical to life-threatening conditions, such as insulin for diabetics or heart medications, consider securing an even longer supply if possible. Additionally, keep a detailed written record of each prescription, including the medication name, dose, frequency, prescribing doctor, and a plan for renewal. This documentation will be invaluable if you need to obtain emergency supplies from a different pharmacy or healthcare provider.

Transporting prescription medications requires careful consideration, especially for bug-in scenarios where you might need to move to a safer location within your home or evacuate entirely. Portable, waterproof, and durable medication containers are essential for protecting your medications during transport. These containers should be easy to carry and discreet for security purposes. Include a small, laminated card or sheet within each container listing the medications, dosages, and prescribing doctor's contact information. This can assist emergency personnel or healthcare providers in understanding your medical needs quickly.

Finally, the disposal of expired or unused medications is an often-overlooked aspect of medication management. Proper disposal is crucial to prevent accidental ingestion or misuse. Many pharmacies offer take-back programs where you can return expired or unused medications safely. Alternatively, follow the FDA guidelines for disposing of medications in household trash by mixing them with an unpalatable substance and placing them in a sealed bag or container.

In essence, the meticulous organization, proper storage, and strategic planning for renewals and disposal form the cornerstone of managing prescription medications for emergency preparedness. By adhering to these practices, you ensure that you and your loved ones have uninterrupted access to essential medications, maintaining health and well-being even in challenging circumstances.

Natural Remedies and Supplements

In the realm of medical preparedness, particularly within the confines of a secure bug-in location, the strategic inclusion of natural remedies and supplements can play a pivotal role in maintaining health and addressing minor ailments. Herbal supplements and natural treatments, revered for their minimal side effects and compatibility with the human body, offer a sustainable approach to bolstering immunity and treating common conditions that may arise during prolonged periods of self-reliance.

Echinacea, a widely recognized immune-boosting herb, stands at the forefront of natural supplements recommended for preparedness strategies. Its properties have been studied for their effectiveness in both preventing and alleviating the symptoms of the common cold, making it an essential component of any home pharmacy. For optimal use, Echinacea supplements should be started at the first sign of cold symptoms and continued for no more than two weeks to maximize its immune-enhancing benefits.

Another cornerstone of natural medical preparedness is the use of elderberry. Elderberry syrup, particularly derived from the Sambucus nigra species, has been documented for its antiviral properties and its ability to shorten the duration of flu symptoms. Incorporating elderberry syrup into your regimen at the onset of flu-like symptoms not only aids in swift recovery but also serves as a preventive measure during peak flu seasons, thanks to its immune-supportive qualities.

For addressing gastrointestinal disturbances, which can be common in stress-induced environments or when dietary habits are altered, ginger and peppermint stand out for their digestive support. Ginger, either in the form of capsules, teas, or fresh root, can significantly alleviate nausea and aid in digestion. Peppermint tea, known for its soothing effect on the gastrointestinal tract, can relieve symptoms of indigestion and irritable bowel syndrome. These natural remedies are not only effective but also offer the advantage of being easily stored and having a long shelf life, making them ideal for inclusion in a bug-in scenario.

Turmeric, with its active compound curcumin, is another invaluable addition to the natural health arsenal. Its anti-inflammatory and antioxidant properties make it beneficial for managing pain and inflammation, common complaints that may not always warrant medical intervention but can significantly affect quality of life. Integrating turmeric into daily routines, either as a supplement or through dietary sources, can contribute to overall well-being and resilience against chronic conditions.

In the context of stress management and sleep disturbances—two significant challenges in high-stress or emergency situations—valerian root and melatonin supplements can provide natural relief. Valerian root, used in traditional medicine for its sedative qualities, can improve sleep quality without the grogginess associated with over-the-counter sleep aids. Melatonin, a hormone that regulates sleep-wake cycles, can be used judiciously to correct sleep patterns disrupted by stress or changes in the environment.

It's imperative to approach the use of herbal supplements and natural remedies with a discerning eye, recognizing that while they offer numerous benefits, they are not a panacea and should be integrated into a broader strategy of health and wellness. Consulting with healthcare professionals, particularly in the context of existing medical conditions or when using prescription medications, ensures that natural remedies complement rather than complicate medical preparedness efforts.

Incorporating these natural remedies and supplements into your bug-in medical preparedness plan not only diversifies your healthcare options but also aligns with a holistic approach to well-being, ensuring that you and your loved ones remain resilient and capable of addressing minor health concerns with confidence and efficacy.

Managing Health Conditions Independently

Recognizing and Treating Common Ailments

Materials
- Comprehensive first aid kit including:
- Antiseptics (isopropyl alcohol, hydrogen peroxide)
- Variety of bandages (adhesive bandages, gauze pads, butterfly closures)
- Over-the-counter medications (pain relievers, antihistamines, antacids)
- Prescription medications specific to family members' needs
- Thermometer
- Tweezers and scissors
- Elastic wraps and splints
- Instruction booklet on first aid procedures
- Digital blood pressure monitor
- Glucose monitoring kit (for families with diabetic members)
- Rehydration salts
- Antidiarrheal medication
- Oral rehydration solution packets
- Hot and cold packs
- Protective gloves

Tools
- Smartphone or computer with internet access for symptom research
- Notepad and pen for tracking symptoms and treatments
- Medical reference book or app for quick information

Step-by-step instructions

1. **Identify Symptoms:** When a family member feels unwell, start by carefully noting all symptoms they're experiencing. Use a notepad and pen to keep track of their symptoms, including their severity and when they started.

2. **Consult Reliable Sources:** Use your smartphone or computer to research the symptoms on reputable medical websites or consult a medical reference book to understand potential causes. Always cross-reference information to ensure accuracy.

3. **Check the First Aid Kit:** Open your comprehensive first aid kit to gather materials needed for treating the identified symptoms. Ensure you have all necessary items before beginning any treatment.

4. **Follow First Aid Procedures:** Refer to the instruction booklet included in your first aid kit for guidance on treating common ailments like cuts, burns, or sprains. Follow the steps carefully, using the materials you've prepared.

5. **Use Over-the-Counter Medications Wisely:** For minor ailments like headaches, allergies, or stomach issues, use the over-the-counter medications from your kit. Ensure you're familiar with the correct dosages and any potential side effects.

6. **Monitor Vital Signs:** For more serious conditions, use the digital blood pressure monitor and thermometer to keep track of the patient's vital signs. Record these measurements to monitor trends over time.

7. **Stay Hydrated:** In cases of fever or gastrointestinal issues, hydration is key. Use oral rehydration solution packets mixed with clean water to prevent dehydration.

8. **Apply Hot or Cold Packs:** For injuries such as sprains or muscle strains, use hot or cold packs from your kit to reduce swelling and relieve pain. Remember, ice should not be applied directly to the skin and should be used for only 20 minutes at a time.

9. **Seek Professional Help if Necessary:** If symptoms persist or worsen, do not hesitate to seek professional medical advice. Always err on the side of caution, especially if the patient is very young, elderly, or has pre-existing health conditions.

Safety tips
- Always check expiration dates on medications and replace any expired items promptly.
- Wash your hands thoroughly before and after administering first aid to prevent infection.
- Wear protective gloves when dealing with blood or bodily fluids.
- Never attempt to treat severe medical conditions on your own. Seek professional medical assistance immediately.

Maintenance
- Regularly check and restock your first aid kit to ensure you have all necessary supplies on hand.
- Keep your first aid kit in a known, easily accessible location.
- Update prescription medications as needed, ensuring you have an adequate supply for family members with chronic conditions.

Difficulty rating ★★☆☆☆

Variations

- For households with specific medical needs (e.g., allergies, asthma), include additional items like epinephrine injectors or inhalers in your first aid kit.
- Customize your first aid kit based on your family's activities. For example, if you frequently hike or camp, include items like snake bite kits or water purification tablets.

Long-Term Management of Chronic Conditions

Managing chronic conditions such as diabetes, heart disease, and other persistent illnesses requires a comprehensive and proactive approach, especially in scenarios where access to traditional medical facilities and professionals might be limited or entirely absent. The key to effectively managing these conditions off-grid lies in meticulous planning, education, and self-sufficiency.

For individuals with diabetes, maintaining a stable blood glucose level becomes paramount. This involves securing a reliable supply of necessary medications, such as insulin, which may require refrigeration. Utilizing portable, solar-powered coolers can offer a viable solution for storing insulin safely. Moreover, a thorough understanding of carbohydrate counting and the impact of various foods on blood glucose levels is essential. Regular monitoring with a blood glucose meter, ensuring an ample supply of test strips and lancets, and having a ketone testing kit for type 1 diabetes are critical components of diabetes management. It's also beneficial to stockpile syringes or pen needles, depending on your method of insulin delivery.

Heart disease management focuses on maintaining a heart-healthy lifestyle even in an off-grid setting. This includes a diet low in sodium and saturated fats, coupled with regular physical activity tailored to one's specific condition and capabilities. Ensuring an adequate supply of prescribed medications such as beta-blockers, ACE inhibitors, or statins is crucial, as is the ability to monitor blood pressure with a reliable, manually operated blood pressure cuff. Recognizing the symptoms of heart distress and having a plan for emergency response, including the use of aspirin in the event of a suspected heart attack, is a vital part of preparedness.

For all chronic conditions, creating a detailed management plan involves documenting medication dosages, schedules, and any necessary lifestyle adjustments. This plan should be reviewed and updated regularly in consultation with healthcare providers to adapt to any changes in the condition or available resources. Education plays a critical role; individuals should seek to understand their conditions thoroughly, recognizing signs of potential complications and knowing when and how to take action.

Compiling a comprehensive medical reference library, including books and reliable online resources that can be accessed offline, provides a valuable tool for managing health conditions when professional medical advice is not readily available. Additionally, cultivating a network of support within your community can offer assistance and share the burden of managing chronic conditions, providing both practical help and emotional support.

In terms of equipment and supplies, prioritizing the most critical items for your condition is essential. For example, those with respiratory issues might focus on securing a backup power source for oxygen concentrators or nebulizers. The use of detailed labels and organized storage systems can ensure that supplies are easily accessible and that their expiration dates are monitored to keep the stockpile current.

Lastly, mental health and stress management are integral to managing chronic conditions, particularly in challenging environments. Techniques such as deep breathing, meditation, and maintaining social connections can help mitigate stress, which is often a significant factor in exacerbating chronic health issues.

By adopting a meticulous and informed approach to managing chronic conditions, individuals can maintain their health and quality of life even in off-grid or survival situations. This proactive stance empowers individuals, transforming them from survivors to strategists in their health care management.

Emergency Medical Procedures

In the realm of medical preparedness, especially when isolated from immediate professional help, knowing how to perform key emergency medical procedures can be the difference between life and death. These procedures, including **CPR (Cardiopulmonary Resuscitation)**, treating severe wounds, and handling fractures, are foundational skills that every individual aiming to protect and provide for their loved ones in crisis situations should master.

Starting with **CPR**, this life-saving technique is crucial in situations where someone's breathing or heartbeat has stopped. When performing CPR, the goal is to mimic the heart's pumping action by compressing the chest, which helps circulate blood and oxygen throughout the body, and providing breaths if trained to do so. The recommended method involves placing the heel of one hand on the center of the chest, placing the other hand on top, and pressing down hard and fast, at a rate of 100 to 120 compressions per minute. Remember, CPR for adults differs slightly from CPR for children and infants, primarily in the force of compressions and the method of providing breaths, making it essential to familiarize oneself with these differences.

Moving on to **treating severe wounds**, the primary aim is to stop bleeding and prevent infection. In cases of heavy bleeding, apply direct pressure with a clean cloth or bandage. If the bleeding does not stop, consider applying pressure to the nearest artery. Use a tourniquet only as a last resort when direct pressure cannot control the bleeding, and professional help is not immediately available. After managing the bleeding, clean the wound with clean water, apply an antibiotic ointment if available, and cover it with a sterile dressing. It's crucial to monitor the wound for signs of infection, such as increased redness, swelling, or a pus-like discharge.

Handling **fractures** requires immobilizing the injured area to prevent further injury. If you suspect a bone is broken, stabilize the limb using splints made from rigid materials like wood or metal, padding them to avoid skin damage. The splint should extend beyond the joints above and below the fracture. Secure the splint with bandages or cloth strips, ensuring they're tight enough to hold but not cut off circulation. Always check for signs of reduced blood flow, such as coldness, numbness, or a blue tint to the skin beyond the injury. In cases of suspected neck or back injuries, avoid moving the person unless absolutely necessary to prevent further harm.

These emergency medical procedures are not substitutes for professional medical care but are critical interim measures that can save lives or prevent conditions from worsening until help arrives. Mastery of these techniques comes from hands-on practice, ideally under the guidance of professionals through courses offered by organizations like the American Red Cross or the American Heart Association. Investing time in learning and regularly refreshing these skills ensures you're prepared to act confidently and effectively in emergencies, embodying the proactive and protective ethos at the heart of this guide.

Psychological First Aid in Crises

In the midst of a crisis, the psychological impact on individuals can be as significant as the physical dangers. The ability to provide psychological first aid (PFA) becomes a critical skill set, enabling you to offer immediate support to those experiencing mental stress and emotional distress. This form of aid is designed to reduce the initial distress caused by traumatic events and to foster short- and long-term adaptive functioning and coping. Recognizing the signs of mental stress is the first step in effective PFA. These signs can vary widely among individuals but often include changes in behavior, such as withdrawal from social interactions, increased irritability, or difficulty sleeping. Physical symptoms might also manifest, including fatigue, headaches, and stomachaches, which are psychosomatic responses to stress.

To address these issues, begin by ensuring that the affected individual feels safe and comfortable. Create an environment that promotes calm and reassurance without overwhelming them with information or expectations. It's essential to listen actively, allowing them to share their feelings and experiences without judgment. Acknowledge their distress and validate their feelings, reinforcing that their reactions are normal responses to abnormal events. Offering practical assistance with basic needs or concerns can also help reduce immediate stress and foster a sense of security.

In terms of specific techniques, grounding exercises can be particularly effective in managing acute stress reactions. These exercises help individuals focus on the present moment and can reduce feelings of panic or dissociation. Simple strategies include deep breathing exercises, identifying objects in their surroundings, or engaging in a conversation about non-distressing topics. Encourage them to focus on their breathing, take note of their environment using their senses, or participate in simple, grounding conversations. These methods can help distract from overwhelming emotions and bring their attention back to the present.

Another critical aspect of PFA is encouraging the use of existing support systems. Remind individuals of their strengths and the resources available to them, including friends, family, and community networks. Reinforcing these connections can provide emotional support and practical assistance, enhancing resilience and the capacity to cope with the crisis.

For those with pre-existing mental health conditions, it's crucial to encourage continuity in treatment when possible. This might involve helping them to access medication, facilitating contact with mental health professionals, or providing information about online support resources and telehealth services.

In all interactions, it's important to maintain confidentiality and respect privacy, ensuring that individuals feel safe and supported in sharing their experiences. Remember, the goal of PFA is not to provide therapy or to solve all of the individual's problems but rather to offer support and stabilization, and to facilitate access to additional services if and when they are needed.

Lastly, it's vital to recognize when someone may need more specialized mental health intervention. Signs that professional help may be needed include persistent inability to perform daily tasks, intense or prolonged distress, and dangerous or self-harming behaviors. In such cases, refer them to mental health professionals or emergency services for further evaluation and treatment.

By applying these principles of psychological first aid, you can play a crucial role in helping individuals navigate the emotional challenges of a crisis, supporting their journey towards recovery and resilience.

Video BONUS

Chapter 8: Crisis Communication and Networking

Emergency Communication Systems

Communication Needs in a Crisis

In the heat of a crisis, the ability to communicate effectively becomes a lifeline, not just a convenience. Whether facing a natural disaster, a power outage, or a security threat, the types of emergencies you might encounter can vary widely, necessitating a robust and versatile communication plan. The first step in establishing this plan is to assess your communication requirements meticulously, considering the nature of potential emergencies and the environment you're operating within. This assessment should encompass both the means of communication at your disposal and the content of the messages you might need to convey.

For instance, in a scenario where cellular networks are down due to a natural disaster, alternative communication methods such as **HAM radios** or **satellite phones** may become essential. These tools can provide a critical link to the outside world, allowing you to receive updates on the situation and communicate with emergency services or family members outside the affected area. It's crucial to familiarize yourself with the operation of these devices in advance, ensuring that batteries are charged and that all family members know how to use them.

Moreover, the content of your communications must be clear, concise, and actionable. In an emergency, every second counts, and there's no room for ambiguity. This means having pre-established codes or signals that can convey complex information quickly and unambiguously. For example, a simple text message like "Code Red" could inform family members that they need to immediately move to a pre-determined safe location.

Another critical aspect of your communication plan is redundancy. Relying on a single method of communication is a common pitfall that can lead to complete communication failure when that method is compromised. Therefore, your plan should include multiple layers of redundancy. This could mean having both electronic and non-electronic means of communication, such as a whistle or a brightly colored flag to signal for help if electronic devices fail.

In addition to planning for outbound communication, you must also consider how you will receive information from external sources. This could involve setting up a battery-powered or hand-crank radio to listen to emergency broadcasts if the power is out. Knowing which local stations to tune into for emergency updates or having a list of online resources that can be accessed via satellite connection can provide you with vital information about the crisis at hand and help you make informed decisions.

Lastly, the psychological aspect of communication cannot be overlooked. In times of crisis, maintaining a sense of connection and normalcy is crucial for mental health. This means setting up regular check-ins with family members, both within the household and with those who may be elsewhere. These check-ins can serve the dual purpose of keeping everyone informed of the situation and providing emotional support, helping to reduce anxiety and maintain morale.

By taking a detailed, methodical approach to assessing your communication needs and planning accordingly, you can ensure that you and your loved ones remain connected and informed, no matter what emergencies you may face. This proactive stance not only enhances your ability to respond effectively to crises but also empowers each family member, reinforcing the collective resilience of your household.

Choosing Emergency Communication Devices

In the realm of emergency preparedness, selecting the right communication devices is paramount to maintaining a lifeline during crises. The landscape of communication technology offers a variety of tools, each with its unique advantages and applications in emergency scenarios. This section delves into the specifics of radios (HAM, GMRS, FRS), satellite phones, and mobile phones, providing guidance on evaluating and choosing the most suitable options for your needs.

Starting with radios, HAM (Amateur Radio) stands out for its versatility and range. HAM radios operate on a wide spectrum of frequencies, allowing for long-distance communication even in the absence of traditional networks. To operate a HAM radio, one must obtain a license by passing a test that covers basic regulations, operating practices, and electronics theory. The investment in learning and licensing is offset by the unparalleled capability of HAM radios to facilitate communication in remote areas, during natural disasters, and when other systems are down. For families, acquiring a dual-band HAM radio, capable of operating on VHF (Very High Frequency) and UHF (Ultra High Frequency) bands, ensures broader access to both local and distant emergency communication networks.

GMRS (General Mobile Radio Service) radios offer a more accessible, albeit shorter-range, alternative. With a straightforward licensing process that doesn't require a test, GMRS radios can be an excellent option for family communication plans. They operate on specific frequencies designated by the FCC, providing clear and reliable two-way communication over several miles, depending on the terrain and the presence of repeaters. When choosing GMRS radios, look for models with integrated NOAA (National Oceanic and Atmospheric Administration) channels to receive real-time weather alerts, enhancing your situational awareness during emergencies.

FRS (Family Radio Service) radios are the most user-friendly option, requiring no license and offering a simple, out-of-the-box solution for short-range communication. Ideal for coordinating with family members during outings or in situations where cell service is unreliable, FRS radios are limited to lower power than GMRS, which constrains their range but also makes them safe and easy for all ages to use. For emergency kits, select FRS radios with built-in emergency features such as SOS signals or flashlight functions to maximize their utility in crisis situations.

Satellite phones bridge the gap when terrestrial networks are unavailable or destroyed. Unlike traditional mobile phones that rely on cell towers, satellite phones communicate directly with orbiting satellites, providing coverage in the most remote locations. When evaluating satellite phones, consider the coverage area offered by the provider, ensuring it encompasses your region and typical travel destinations. Subscription plans vary, with options ranging from pay-as-you-go to monthly contracts; assess your communication needs and budget to find a suitable plan. A critical feature to look for in a satellite phone is the ability to send and receive SMS messages and emails, facilitating communication with emergency services and loved ones even when voice calls are not feasible.

Mobile phones, while ubiquitous, are often rendered useless in disasters due to network congestion or infrastructure damage. However, they remain a critical tool in emergency preparedness. Smartphones equipped with GPS, maps, and emergency apps can provide vital information and communication capabilities in the initial stages of a crisis. Preparing your mobile phone for emergencies involves keeping a list of essential contacts, downloading offline maps, and investing in portable power banks to ensure your device remains charged. Leveraging text messages, which often get through even when voice calls cannot, can be a lifeline in communicating with family and emergency services.

In conclusion, the choice of communication devices for emergency preparedness is a multifaceted decision that hinges on understanding the specific capabilities and limitations of each option. Balancing the need for long-range communication with the practicalities of licensing, ease of use, and cost, requires a strategic approach. Equip your household with a combination of devices, ensuring redundancy and versatility in your communication plan. Remember, the best communication device is the one that works when you need it most, so prioritize reliability and familiarity for all users in your family.

Communication Equipment Maintenance

Setting up and maintaining communication equipment is a critical component of ensuring your home is prepared for any crisis. This involves not just selecting the right devices but also installing, configuring, and regularly maintaining them to guarantee they are operational when most needed. Radios, including HAM, GMRS, and FRS, along with satellite phones and even traditional mobile phones, form the backbone of a robust emergency communication system. Each device has its specific setup and maintenance requirements, which we will delve into, ensuring you can rely on these tools when conventional communication networks might fail.

For **radios**, the installation process begins with understanding the frequency and licensing requirements. HAM radios, for example, require a license to operate on certain frequencies. Once you have the necessary permissions, the next step is to configure your radio. This involves programming in the frequencies you intend to use, which can be done manually or with software, depending on the radio model. It's essential to include local emergency frequencies, as well as national weather channels, to stay informed during crises. Regular maintenance includes checking the battery life and ensuring all connections are secure. For battery-powered radios, consider using rechargeable batteries and have a solar charger on hand as a sustainable power source.

Satellite phones offer a reliable communication method when cellular networks are down. When setting up a satellite phone, ensure it is registered and activated according to the service provider's instructions. Test the phone in different locations around your property to identify areas with the strongest signal. Satellite phones rely on direct line of sight to satellites, so clear skies and minimal obstructions are crucial for optimal use. Maintenance for these devices involves regularly charging the battery, updating the software as recommended by the manufacturer, and protecting the phone from extreme temperatures and water exposure.

For **mobile phones**, while they may not be reliable in every crisis situation due to network congestion or damage to infrastructure, they can still play a role in your communication plan. Keep your phone's software updated to ensure you have the latest features and security patches. Use protective cases to guard against damage and have backup power sources, like power banks or solar chargers, to keep your phone charged during extended power outages. Additionally, consider installing emergency communication apps that can send distress signals or share your location with family members even when cellular networks are down.

Maintenance tips for all communication devices include:
- Regularly testing equipment to ensure functionality. This means making test calls or transmissions at scheduled intervals.
- Keeping devices clean and dry, as moisture and dirt can impair functionality.
- Storing devices and their accessories in easily accessible, yet secure locations to prevent damage and ensure they are ready to use when needed.

- Updating any necessary software and staying informed about changes in communication regulations or frequency allocations that might affect your equipment.

In summary, the key to effective crisis communication lies in the careful selection, setup, and maintenance of your communication devices. By taking the time to understand the capabilities and requirements of each piece of equipment and by committing to regular maintenance, you ensure that you and your loved ones remain connected in any emergency.

Backup Communication Strategies

In the realm of crisis communication, redundancy is not just a precaution; it's a necessity. Establishing a robust backup communication strategy ensures that, even in the face of primary system failures, you remain connected with the outside world, coordinating with emergency services, and keeping in touch with your loved ones. The foundation of a solid backup plan lies in diversifying your communication tools and methods to create a fail-safe system that can withstand various disaster scenarios.

One effective strategy is to integrate a mix of high-tech and low-tech communication options. For instance, while digital communication devices like satellite phones and HAM radios offer unparalleled connectivity in many emergency situations, their reliability can be compromised by power outages, network overloads, or equipment failure. To counteract these vulnerabilities, incorporating low-tech options such as signaling mirrors, whistles, and even pre-arranged visual signals using flags or lights can provide a critical means of communication when more advanced technologies fail.

Moreover, establishing a cache of written messages or letters in a waterproof, easily accessible container can serve as a last-resort communication method with rescue teams or other survivors. This method, while primitive, ensures that your status, location, and needs are documented and can be communicated even without direct contact.

For redundancy, every household member should be familiar with at least two methods of emergency communication. Training and drills that include scenarios where primary communication tools have failed will ensure that each person can competently switch to alternate methods under stress. For example, practice using a hand-crank emergency radio to receive information when there's no electricity, and ensure everyone knows how to operate it.

In addition to diversifying communication methods, it's crucial to maintain a network of contacts that extends beyond your immediate area. Establishing a communication link with a trusted individual or family outside your region can provide a relay point for messages and updates. This external contact can be invaluable in situations where local communication networks are down, allowing you to relay messages through them to emergency services or other family members.

The physical components of your backup communication plan—such as batteries, chargers, and other accessories—should be stored in EMP-resistant containers to protect against electromagnetic pulses that could render electronic devices useless. For power sources, consider solar chargers, hand-crank generators, and battery banks to ensure your devices remain operational without access to the grid.

In essence, a comprehensive backup communication strategy encompasses a layered approach that combines multiple communication methods, regular training on their use, and the establishment of a broader communication network. This approach not only prepares you for a wide range of scenarios but also instills a level of resilience and adaptability in your emergency preparedness plan. By prioritizing communication redundancy, you safeguard your ability to stay informed, coordinate with others, and ultimately increase your chances of survival and recovery in the aftermath of a crisis.

Video BONUS

Chapter 9: Essential Survival Gear

Navy SEAL Gear for Home Defense

Firearms for Home Defense

Selecting the right firearms and ammunition for home defense is a critical decision that requires careful consideration of various factors including reliability, ease of use, and the specific needs of your household. When it comes to safeguarding your loved ones and property, the goal is to choose weapons that can be effectively managed by all capable members of the family while providing the necessary stopping power to neutralize potential threats.

For home defense, the shotgun is a popular choice due to its versatility and formidable stopping power at close ranges. The 12-gauge pump-action shotgun, in particular, is recommended for its reliability and ease of use. Models like the Mossberg 500 or the Remington 870 are renowned for their durability and have been trusted by law enforcement and military personnel for decades. These shotguns offer the advantage of being effective even when using less-lethal ammunition, such as rubber bullets, which can be a consideration for those concerned about the potential for fatal outcomes in a home defense scenario.

Handguns are another vital component of a home defense arsenal. They provide the advantage of being easily maneuverable in tight spaces, which is a common scenario during a home invasion. For those with limited experience, a semi-automatic pistol in 9mm caliber is often recommended due to its manageable recoil, relatively high capacity, and the widespread availability of ammunition. Models like the Glock 17 or 19, Sig Sauer P320, and Smith & Wesson M&P Shield are praised for their reliability, ease of use, and ergonomic designs that accommodate a wide range of hand sizes.

Rifles, particularly those in .223/5.56 caliber such as the AR-15, offer precision and the capacity for longer-range engagement if the situation extends beyond the confines of the home. The AR-15 platform is noted for its modularity, allowing users to customize their weapon to fit their specific needs, including home defense. Lightweight, with manageable recoil, the AR-15 can be equipped with various optics and accessories to enhance its effectiveness. It's important to choose ammunition designed for home defense, such as hollow-point rounds, which are engineered to expand upon impact, reducing the risk of over-penetration and collateral damage.

In terms of ammunition, it is crucial to stockpile a sufficient quantity to ensure readiness for prolonged situations. For shotguns, a mix of buckshot for its stopping power and birdshot for less-lethal options can be considered. Handgun and rifle owners should prioritize hollow-point ammunition for its effectiveness in stopping threats while minimizing risks to bystanders through over-penetration.

Storage and accessibility are paramount concerns when incorporating firearms into your home defense strategy. Weapons should be stored securely to prevent unauthorized access, especially by children, but be readily accessible to authorized users in an emergency. Biometric safes and quick-access lock boxes are recommended for storing handguns, while larger safes can accommodate shotguns and rifles. Regular training and familiarization with all firearms in the household are essential to ensure that in a crisis, every capable family member can safely and effectively use the weapons.

By selecting the appropriate firearms and ammunition, you equip your household to respond decisively and effectively to potential threats. This preparation, combined with regular practice and safety education, forms the cornerstone of a robust home defense strategy that prioritizes the protection of your loved ones while minimizing risks to their safety and well-being.

Non-Lethal Defense Options

In the realm of home defense, the emphasis often leans heavily towards lethal means of protection, such as firearms. However, a comprehensive security strategy also includes non-lethal defense options, which can be pivotal in situations where lethal force is not warranted or legally permissible. Non-lethal tools offer a spectrum of defense capabilities, allowing you to incapacitate or deter an intruder without causing permanent harm. Among these tools, **pepper spray**, **tasers**, and **impact weapons** like expandable batons, stand out for their effectiveness and ease of use.

Pepper spray, also known as OC (oleoresin capsicum) spray, is a potent chemical agent that irritates the eyes to cause tears, pain, and temporary blindness. Its effectiveness lies in its ability to incapacitate an attacker from a distance, providing a window of opportunity for escape or to call for help. When selecting pepper spray, opt for models that offer a range of at least 10 feet, ensuring you can maintain a safe distance from an assailant. Look for sprays with a high OC concentration and a UV marking dye, which can help in the identification of the assailant after the fact. It's crucial to familiarize yourself with the operation of the pepper spray device—practice quick draws and aim with a training canister to ensure readiness in a high-stress situation.

Tasers and **stun guns** offer another layer of non-lethal defense, delivering an electric shock that temporarily disrupts muscle function without causing permanent injury. While both devices operate on the same basic principle, tasers can be used from a distance, whereas stun guns require direct contact. For home defense, a taser is preferable due to its range, allowing you to maintain distance from an intruder. When choosing a taser, consider models with a laser sight for accuracy and models that can deliver multiple shocks if necessary. Training is essential to effectively employ a taser under pressure, so invest in a training course and practice regularly to build confidence and proficiency.

Impact weapons, such as expandable batons, provide a means of defense that requires close proximity but can be highly effective in trained hands. An expandable baton offers the advantage of being compact and easily stored or carried, then quickly extended for use. The key to effective use is training—knowing how to strike effectively and understanding the legal implications of using such a tool for self-defense. Seek out a baton constructed from high-grade steel or aluminum for durability and reliability. Training courses in baton use can provide the necessary skills to use this tool effectively while minimizing the risk to yourself and others.

For all non-lethal defense options, legal knowledge is as crucial as practical skill. Familiarize yourself with state and local laws regarding the possession and use of these tools. Some jurisdictions may have restrictions or require permits for items like pepper spray and tasers. Additionally, consider the psychological and emotional preparedness required to use these tools under duress. Regular training, both physical and scenario-based, can enhance your readiness to act decisively and responsibly in a crisis.

Incorporating non-lethal defense options into your home security plan offers a balanced approach to protecting yourself and your loved ones. By selecting the right tools, acquiring the necessary training, and understanding the legal landscape, you equip yourself with a range of responses to potential threats. This not only enhances your overall safety but also aligns with a responsible and ethical approach to self-defense.

Home Security Systems

In the realm of home defense, integrating a comprehensive **home security system** is paramount for ensuring the safety and security of your loved ones and property. The foundation of an effective system lies in a triad of components: **alarm systems**, **motion detectors**, and **surveillance cameras**, each serving a distinct role in a layered defense strategy.

Alarm systems act as the central hub of your home security, monitoring various sensors and detectors throughout the property and alerting you to potential breaches. For maximum effectiveness, opt for a system that offers both audible alarms to deter intruders and silent alerts sent directly to your smartphone or a monitoring service. Look for models that include backup power solutions, such as battery reserves, to maintain functionality during power outages. Integration with smart home technologies can also provide enhanced control, allowing you to arm or disarm the system remotely and receive real-time notifications of any security events.

Motion detectors are the eyes of your security system, providing early warning of unauthorized movement within specific areas of your property. When selecting motion detectors, consider units that offer pet immunity to avoid false alarms triggered by household pets. Placement is critical; install detectors in high-traffic areas such as hallways, stairwells, and near entry points. For outdoor coverage, choose weather-resistant models with adjustable sensitivity settings to minimize false alarms caused by wildlife or environmental factors.

Surveillance cameras serve as both a deterrent to potential intruders and a means of gathering evidence in the event of a security breach. Today's market offers a wide range of cameras suited for home defense, including high-definition, night vision, and motion-activated models. For exterior surveillance, select cameras with robust weatherproofing and infrared night vision capabilities to ensure clear footage regardless of lighting conditions. Inside the home, discreet cameras can monitor entryways and common areas. Wireless technology allows for flexible placement and easy integration with existing home networks, enabling remote viewing of live feeds from smartphones or tablets.

When configuring your surveillance setup, consider both fixed and pan-tilt-zoom (PTZ) cameras. Fixed cameras provide constant coverage of specific areas, while PTZ models can be remotely controlled to survey a wider area. Strategic placement is key to eliminating blind spots and ensuring comprehensive coverage of your property. Ensure cameras are positioned to cover all entry points, including doors and windows, as well as driveways and other potential access routes.

To enhance the efficacy of your home security system, incorporate **lighting** with motion detection capabilities around the perimeter of your home. Well-lit areas not only deter potential intruders but also improve the quality of surveillance footage. Additionally, integrating your security system with a **smart home automation system** can provide advanced features such as scheduled lighting, simulated occupancy through television or radio timers, and automatic locking of doors and windows.

In selecting components for your home security system, prioritize products from reputable manufacturers with a proven track record of reliability and customer support. Regular testing and maintenance of the system are essential to ensure all components are functioning correctly and to identify any potential issues before they compromise your security.

By meticulously selecting and strategically deploying alarm systems, motion detectors, and surveillance cameras, you can create a robust home security system that not only deters potential intruders but also provides a critical line of defense in protecting your family and property. With the right setup, you transform your home into a secure fortress, granting you peace of mind knowing that your loved ones are safeguarded against potential threats.

Tactical Gear for Home Security

In the realm of home defense, tactical gear plays a pivotal role in ensuring the safety and security of your loved ones. Drawing inspiration from Navy SEALs, who are renowned for their rigorous standards and exceptional gear, one can significantly enhance their home defense capabilities. The selection of tactical gear such as body armor, helmets, and additional protective equipment is not merely about having tools at your disposal; it's about creating a comprehensive defense strategy that can adapt to various threats and scenarios.

Body armor, for instance, is a critical component for personal protection. When selecting body armor, consider the level of protection it offers, which is categorized from Level IIA, which provides the least protection, to Level IV, which can stop armor-piercing rifle rounds. For home defense purposes, a Level IIIA vest is often recommended as it offers protection against most handgun rounds while still being relatively lightweight and flexible. It's essential to ensure that the body armor fits properly, covering vital organs while allowing for mobility and comfort during prolonged periods of wear.

Helmets are another crucial piece of tactical gear, designed to protect against head injuries from blunt force trauma and ballistic threats. A high-cut ballistic helmet offers a balance between protection and functionality, allowing for the addition of communication equipment, night vision devices, and other accessories. Look for helmets that meet NIJ ballistic protection standards and consider the weight and adjustability to ensure a secure and comfortable fit.

Additional protective gear, such as knee pads, elbow pads, and tactical gloves, provides extra layers of defense against physical harm during a home invasion or when securing your perimeter. These items should be chosen for their durability, flexibility, and the protection they offer against impacts and abrasions. Tactical gloves, in particular, should offer a firm grip, dexterity, and, if possible, cut resistance, to handle weapons and tools effectively.

When assembling your tactical gear, it's also wise to include a tactical flashlight with a high lumen output and strobe function. This can disorient intruders and aid in navigation and threat identification in low-light conditions. A multi-tool is another indispensable item, providing various functions in one compact tool, from cutting and sawing to screwing and measuring, which can be crucial in emergency repair situations or when modifying your home's defenses.

Incorporating tactical gear into your home defense strategy requires careful consideration of your specific needs, potential threats, and the environment you're preparing to defend. Each piece of gear should be evaluated not just on its protective qualities but on how it integrates with other defensive measures you have in place. Training and familiarity with your gear are just as important as the gear itself, ensuring that you can deploy it effectively under stress. Regularly review and update your tactical gear setup to adapt to evolving threats and to incorporate new advancements in protective technology.

By adopting a strategic approach to selecting and utilizing tactical gear inspired by Navy SEALs, you can significantly enhance your ability to protect your home and loved ones. This gear, when combined with a solid home defense plan, physical and mental preparedness, and situational awareness, forms a robust defense framework that can deter, withstand, and overcome a wide range of threats.

Must-Have Tools for Crisis Scenarios

Essential Cutting Tools for Emergencies

In the realm of emergency preparedness, the selection and use of cutting tools are paramount for both survival and defensive scenarios. The right cutting tool can mean the difference between being able to quickly adapt and respond to a crisis or finding oneself at a significant disadvantage. Knives, multi-tools, and axes each serve distinct purposes and come with their own sets of advantages and considerations for use in various situations.

Knives are perhaps the most versatile and essential tools in any emergency kit. A fixed-blade knife, with a blade length of 4 to 6 inches, offers a balance of portability and functionality, making it suitable for a wide range of tasks from self-defense to food preparation. The choice of steel in a knife is critical; high-carbon steel blades, for instance, retain sharpness longer but may require more maintenance to prevent rust, whereas stainless steel variants offer rust resistance at the potential cost of more frequent sharpening. The handle should provide a secure grip even in wet conditions, with materials like G-10 or textured rubber being preferred for their durability and reliability.

Multi-tools embody the principle of multifunctionality, combining several tools in one compact package. A quality multi-tool can include pliers, wire cutters, scissors, a knife blade, screwdrivers, and sometimes specialized tools like a saw or can opener. When choosing a multi-tool, look for one constructed from high-grade stainless steel to ensure longevity and rust resistance. The individual tools should lock into place when fully deployed to prevent accidental closure during use. Consider the types of tasks you anticipate needing to perform most frequently to guide your selection of a multi-tool with the right combination of features.

Axes, while more niche than knives and multi-tools, are indispensable for specific tasks such as chopping wood for fire or breaking through barriers in rescue situations. A tactical axe with a lightweight, fiberglass or metal handle and a carbon steel head offers a good mix of durability and efficiency. The length of the axe should be chosen based on its intended use; a shorter handle (around 14 to 18 inches) provides more control and is suitable for carrying in a pack, whereas a longer handle can increase the force delivered in a swing but at the cost of increased weight and bulk.

When integrating cutting tools into your emergency preparedness plans, consider not only the functionality of each tool but also its maintenance requirements. Regularly inspect tools for signs of wear or damage, and keep blades sharp and clean to ensure they are ready for use when needed. Lubricate moving parts in multi-tools and axes to prevent rust and ensure smooth operation. Additionally, practice with your tools to become proficient in their use; familiarity with your equipment can significantly enhance your effectiveness in emergency situations.

Storage and accessibility are also critical considerations. Keep your cutting tools in a designated spot within your emergency kit or bug-in location, protected from the elements yet easily reachable in a hurry. For those carrying a knife or multi-tool on their person, a sheath or pouch that allows for quick, one-handed access can be invaluable in a crisis.

By carefully selecting and maintaining a set of cutting tools tailored to your specific needs and ensuring you are skilled in their use, you can significantly bolster your preparedness for a wide range of emergency scenarios. Whether it's performing routine tasks around your bug-in location, responding to an immediate threat, or facilitating your survival in the wilderness, the right cutting tools are indispensable components of any comprehensive emergency plan.

Fire-Starting Tools

In the context of crisis scenarios, the ability to start a fire can be pivotal for survival, providing warmth, light, and a means to cook food or purify water. The selection of fire-starting tools must be approached with precision, ensuring reliability under various conditions, from wet weather to high-altitude cold. The cornerstone of an effective fire-starting kit includes a balanced assortment of immediate ignition tools and sustainable fire maintenance items.

Firstly, magnesium fire starters stand out for their durability and effectiveness, even when damp. A magnesium fire starter consists of a block of magnesium with a flint strip. Shavings are scraped off the magnesium block with a knife or a scraping tool into a small pile. Striking the flint edge with a steel scraper directs sparks onto the magnesium shavings, which ignite at temperatures high enough to light even damp kindling. The technique requires practice to perfect the amount of magnesium needed and the force required to generate sparks but offers an unbeatable advantage in adverse conditions.

For a more straightforward approach, waterproof matches are indispensable. These matches are treated with a waterproofing substance, ensuring they remain viable even when exposed to moisture. They often come in durable, watertight containers that double as storage for tinder or other small fire-starting aids. When selecting waterproof matches, opt for those with an extended burn time, providing a longer window to ignite kindling.

Another essential tool is the windproof lighter, a robust solution for instant fire. Unlike traditional lighters, windproof models utilize a jet flame that can withstand strong winds, making them ideal for outdoor use in unpredictable weather. Look for lighters that are refillable and have a transparent reservoir to easily monitor fuel levels. Maintenance is minimal, primarily requiring regular refueling and occasional replacement of the flint.

Beyond ignition tools, carrying a reliable supply of tinder is crucial. Commercially prepared tinder, such as cotton balls impregnated with petroleum jelly, wax-infused wood chips, or fibrous tinder quick tabs, can catch fire quickly and sustain a flame long enough to light larger pieces of kindling. Store these in double-layered zip-lock bags to ensure dryness and ease of access.

Expanding the toolkit, a fire piston represents an ancient yet effective method, utilizing air compression to ignite a small piece of tinder. This tool consists of a hollow cylinder sealed at one end, into which a piston is rapidly inserted. The compressed air within the cylinder heats up to ignite a piece of tinder placed in a recess on the piston's end. Fire pistons require practice to use effectively but serve as a reliable, fuel-less ignition method that can be a conversation starter and a practical tool.

Lastly, an often-overlooked component of the fire-starting kit is a durable metal container or tin, which can serve multiple purposes: storing tinder, protecting fragile components, and even used for making char cloth—a piece of fabric turned into a slow-burning ember starter under low oxygen conditions. A small, hinged tin can withstand the rigors of outdoor life and become an essential part of your fire-making arsenal.

In assembling these tools, the aim is to prepare for a wide range of scenarios, from the need for quick warmth to signal fires or purifying water. Each tool and material has been selected for its proven reliability, ease of use, and effectiveness across conditions. Mastery of these tools not only enhances survival chances but also deepens one's connection with the primal skill of fire-making, echoing the resourcefulness and resilience that crisis scenarios demand.

Water Filtration and Purification Tools

Ensuring access to safe drinking water is a cornerstone of survival in any crisis scenario, making the selection of water filtration and purification tools a critical aspect of preparedness. The right combination of tools not only guarantees the safety of the water but also its availability in sufficient quantities to meet the needs of you and your loved ones. Portable water filters, purification tablets, and boiling kits each play a pivotal role in a comprehensive water treatment strategy, designed to remove or neutralize harmful pathogens and contaminants that can pose serious health risks.

Portable water filters are indispensable for their efficiency and ease of use, providing immediate access to safe drinking water from virtually any source. When selecting a portable water filter, look for models that feature a high-efficiency filter medium, such as hollow fiber membranes or ceramic filters capable of removing bacteria, protozoa, and particulate matter down to 0.2 microns in size. Some filters are also equipped with activated carbon elements to improve taste and remove chemicals. It's important to consider the flow rate of the filter, which is measured in liters per minute, to ensure it meets your hydration needs, especially in group settings. Durability, ease of cleaning, and the capacity of the filter (often measured in thousands of liters before replacement is required) are also key factors. Brands like Sawyer and Katadyn offer various models that cater to different group sizes and filtration needs, with some designed for individual use and others capable of serving entire families.

Purification tablets, such as those containing chlorine dioxide or iodine, offer a lightweight and compact solution for disinfecting water, making them an ideal choice for bug-out bags and emergency kits. These tablets are effective against viruses, bacteria, and cysts, providing a broad spectrum of protection. When using purification tablets, it's crucial to follow the manufacturer's instructions regarding the quantity of tablets needed per volume of water and the required contact time, which can range from 30 minutes to several hours depending on the water temperature and the level of contamination. Although effective, it's worth noting that some individuals may find the taste of water treated with iodine or chlorine dioxide tablets to be off-putting, a drawback that can be mitigated by subsequent filtering through an activated carbon element or by adding flavoring agents after treatment.

Boiling kits, which typically include a portable stove and a durable pot or kettle, represent the most traditional method of water purification. Boiling water for at least one minute (or three minutes at altitudes above 6,500 feet) is effective in killing bacteria, viruses, and protozoa, making it a universally accepted method of water treatment. When assembling a boiling kit, select a lightweight, compact stove that is compatible with multiple fuel sources, and pair it with a stainless steel or anodized aluminum pot that offers a balance between durability and heat efficiency. The inclusion of a lid not only reduces boiling time but also helps conserve fuel, making it a valuable addition to the kit.

Incorporating these tools into your preparedness plan requires not only understanding their individual capabilities and limitations but also recognizing the importance of redundancy in water treatment methods. By equipping yourself with a combination of portable filters, purification tablets, and boiling capabilities, you can ensure that you have the means to produce safe drinking water under a variety of conditions, from on-the-move scenarios to stationary bug-in situations. Regular maintenance and testing of your equipment, along with practicing water treatment techniques, will further enhance your readiness, ensuring that you and your family remain hydrated and healthy regardless of the circumstances you face.

Essential Shelter and Sleeping Gear

In the realm of crisis preparedness, ensuring you have a reliable shelter and sleeping gear is paramount to maintaining safety and warmth in adverse conditions. The selection of tents, tarps, and sleeping bags must be approached with a strategic mindset, focusing on durability, versatility, and ease of use to protect against the elements and ensure a restful night's sleep, which is crucial for maintaining physical strength and mental acuity in survival situations.

Starting with **tents**, the ideal choice is a three-season, freestanding tent that offers a balance between weight and structural integrity. Look for tents with a double-wall construction, which includes a breathable inner layer and a waterproof outer rainfly. This design minimizes condensation build-up inside the tent, keeping the interior dry. The tent's fabric should be a ripstop nylon or polyester with a waterproof rating of at least 3000mm to ensure it can withstand heavy rain. The poles should be made from aluminum rather than fiberglass for a better strength-to-weight ratio and resilience in windy conditions. Opt for tents with a dome or geodesic structure for enhanced stability. Ventilation features such as mesh panels and adjustable vents are crucial to manage airflow and reduce the risk of overheating during warmer nights.

Tarps offer a lightweight and versatile shelter option that can be particularly useful in mild weather conditions or as an additional layer of protection over a tent or sleeping area. Select a tarp made from high-density polyethylene (HDPE) or silnylon for a good balance between durability and weight. The tarp should have reinforced grommets along the edges and at least one in the center to provide multiple setup options, whether strung up between trees or used as a ground cover. The size of the tarp will depend on the intended use; however, a 10x12 foot tarp generally offers sufficient coverage for one to two people plus gear. For added utility, choose a tarp with UV protection and a reflective underside to deflect sunlight and retain heat.

When it comes to **sleeping bags**, selecting the appropriate temperature rating is critical. Choose a sleeping bag rated for temperatures slightly lower than the coldest temperatures you anticipate facing. For most three-season camping scenarios, a bag rated for 20°F (-6°C) is a versatile choice. The insulation type is another important consideration. Synthetic insulation is preferred for its ability to retain heat even when wet and its quick-drying properties, making it suitable for damp environments. Look for sleeping bags with a mummy shape, which is more efficient at retaining body heat due to its closer fit compared to rectangular bags. Features such as a draft collar, insulated zipper baffles, and an adjustable hood can significantly enhance warmth and comfort.

Sleeping pads are an often-overlooked component of sleeping gear that can make a substantial difference in insulation and comfort. A self-inflating foam pad or an air pad with an R-value of 4 or higher is recommended for use in most seasons, providing a good balance between insulation and cushioning. For those seeking the lightest possible setup without sacrificing comfort, an air pad with built-in insulation or a reflective layer offers an effective solution. Ensure the pad's size is compatible with your body dimensions and your sleeping bag to prevent cold spots.

In assembling your shelter and sleeping gear, consider the specific conditions you are preparing for, including the environment, weather, and the duration of your stay. Durability, weather resistance, and thermal efficiency should be the guiding principles in your selection process. Regular maintenance, such as cleaning and properly storing your gear, will extend its lifespan and ensure it's ready when you need it. By meticulously choosing and caring for your shelter and sleeping gear, you equip yourself with a fundamental layer of protection and comfort that can make all the difference in a crisis scenario.

Emergency Communication Tools

In the realm of crisis scenarios, the ability to communicate effectively can mean the difference between safety and peril. Essential communication tools, such as **radios**, **signal mirrors**, and **whistles**, serve as critical lifelines, offering a means to convey distress signals, coordinate with family or rescue teams, and navigate through emergencies with increased chances of survival. Each of these devices plays a unique role in a well-rounded emergency communication plan, and understanding their functions, limitations, and operational protocols is paramount.

Radios, particularly those designed for emergency use, come in various forms, including hand-crank models, solar-powered units, and those compatible with the Family Radio Service (FRS) or General Mobile Radio Service (GMRS) frequencies. Hand-crank and solar-powered radios ensure operability in environments where traditional power sources are unavailable, providing access to NOAA weather alerts and emergency broadcasts. For personal communication, FRS and GMRS radios offer short to medium range connectivity, ideal for staying in touch with family members across different locations within a bug-in scenario. When selecting a radio, prioritize models with multiple power options, including battery operation, to ensure maximum reliability. Look for features such as a built-in flashlight, USB charging ports for other devices, and weather band reception to stay informed about the latest emergency updates.

Signal mirrors are simple yet highly effective tools for signaling rescue teams or communicating over long distances using sunlight reflection. The key to utilizing a signal mirror effectively lies in its ability to reflect light towards a target accurately. Opt for a mirror with a built-in sighting device, which allows for precision signaling by aligning a reflective grid or a hole in the mirror with the intended recipient. Practice is essential to master the technique of flashing the mirror's reflection across vast distances, ensuring that the signal can be seen by search and rescue teams or other members of your group.

Whistles serve as an auditory signal device, capable of emitting loud, piercing sounds that can attract attention in noisy environments or over long distances. The distinct sound of a whistle cuts through ambient noise, making it an invaluable tool for signaling help when visual contact is not possible. Select a whistle designed for emergency use, characterized by a high decibel rating and the ability to function in wet or cold conditions. A pealess design is preferable, as it eliminates the risk of the whistle's pea freezing or sticking in wet conditions, ensuring the whistle remains operational when it's needed most.

Incorporating these communication tools into your emergency preparedness kit requires thoughtful consideration of your environment, the nature of potential crises, and the specific needs of your group or family. Regularly test and maintain these devices to ensure they are in working order and familiarize yourself and your loved ones with their operation. Training sessions that simulate emergency scenarios can be particularly effective in building confidence and competence in using these communication tools under stress.

By equipping yourself with a comprehensive set of communication tools and investing time in learning their proper use, you enhance your ability to navigate emergencies with strategic precision. Radios, signal mirrors, and whistles each offer distinct advantages in transmitting information, coordinating actions, and ultimately, ensuring the safety and security of your loved ones during critical situations.

Stockpiling and Storing Survival Gear

Organizing Your Gear

Efficient organization of survival gear is paramount for ensuring quick access during emergencies, transforming a potentially chaotic situation into a manageable one. The first step in organizing your gear involves categorizing items based on their function and urgency of use. For instance, categorize your gear into medical supplies, food and water, communication devices, and defense tools. Within each category, prioritize items based on how quickly you might need them in an emergency. For example, in your medical supplies, have a separate, easily accessible pouch for life-saving items such as tourniquets, hemostatic agents, and EpiPens, distinguishing them from less urgent supplies like band-aids and antiseptics.

Labeling each category clearly cannot be overstated. Use durable, waterproof labels that are easy to read under low light conditions. Consider also color-coding categories for even faster identification. For instance, use red for medical supplies, blue for water purification tools, and green for food items. This visual cue helps in reducing the time spent searching for items, especially under stress.

For the actual storage of these categorized and labeled items, invest in high-quality, durable containers that are both waterproof and rodent-proof. Containers with stackable features save space and allow for organized storage in limited spaces. Modular storage bins with removable dividers offer flexibility in organizing various sizes and types of gear. Ensure these containers are clearly labeled on multiple sides so identification is possible from any angle.

Implement a systematic layout for storing these containers, keeping those with items you'll need to access quickly, like medical supplies and communication devices, in the most accessible locations. Store items that are less likely to be needed immediately, such as extra clothing or surplus food supplies, in more remote areas of your storage space.

For gear that requires regular maintenance or checks, such as generators, water filters, and fire extinguishers, maintain a detailed log of maintenance schedules and checklists right on the container or in a designated area within your storage space. This practice ensures that all equipment is in working order when needed.

Adopting a digital inventory management system can also enhance your organization. A simple spreadsheet detailing the contents of each container, their expiration dates where applicable, and the last maintenance date for equipment can be invaluable. This system allows for quick checks and ensures that supplies are rotated and maintained as needed, minimizing waste and ensuring readiness.

Incorporating these organization and labeling techniques not only streamlines access to essential gear but also significantly reduces the mental load during an emergency. By mimicking the discipline and systematic approach found in military logistics, you can ensure that your survival gear is ready and accessible when seconds count, without the need for a frantic search or the risk of overlooking critical items.

Gear Storage Best Practices

Selecting the right **storage solutions** for your survival gear is crucial to ensure its longevity and readiness when you need it most. Gear that is improperly stored can suffer from damage due to moisture, pests, and other environmental hazards, rendering it useless in times of crisis. To avoid such pitfalls, it's essential to adopt best practices that safeguard your equipment against these threats.

For moisture control, which is particularly detrimental to metal components and can lead to rust and degradation of materials, using **silica gel packets** within storage containers can significantly reduce humidity levels. These desiccants absorb moisture effectively, keeping the internal environment of your storage containers dry. For larger storage areas, consider a **dehumidifier** to maintain an optimal humidity level, especially in regions prone to high humidity. Ensure that the storage area is well-ventilated to prevent the buildup of condensation.

When it comes to preventing pest infestations, which can wreak havoc on fabric, wood, and other materials, the choice of storage containers becomes paramount. Opt for **airtight, heavy-duty plastic bins** with secure lids to deter rodents and insects. These containers are also beneficial for protecting gear from dust and dirt. For added protection, place **cedar blocks** or **mothballs** within the storage area; these act as natural repellents against moths and other pests without introducing harmful chemicals to your gear.

Another aspect to consider is the **physical location** of your storage. Avoid basements and attics if they are prone to extreme temperature fluctuations or moisture, as these conditions can accelerate the deterioration of stored items. Instead, choose a cool, dry place within your home that maintains a more consistent environment. If using a garage or shed, ensure that it is properly insulated and sealed from the elements.

For items that are sensitive to light, such as food supplies or medical kits, opaque containers offer an additional layer of protection by blocking out harmful UV rays that can degrade the contents over time. Labeling these containers with the contents and the date of storage not only helps in organization but also in rotating supplies to ensure that nothing expires or goes to waste.

Regular inspection of your stored gear is also key to ensuring its longevity. Schedule **quarterly checks** to examine the condition of your items, look for signs of wear or damage, and replace desiccants as needed. This routine maintenance allows you to catch any issues early and take corrective action before your supplies are compromised.

For electronic devices and batteries, consider storing them in **EMP-resistant containers** to protect against electromagnetic pulses that could render them inoperable. Additionally, removing batteries from devices when not in use can prevent corrosion and extend the life of both the batteries and the devices.

By implementing these storage solutions, you're not just organizing your survival gear; you're taking proactive steps to ensure its functionality and reliability for years to come. Protecting your investment from moisture, pests, and environmental damage is essential in maintaining a state of readiness, ensuring that when the time comes, your gear is in optimal condition to support your survival strategy.

Long-Term Storage Considerations

Ensuring the longevity and readiness of survival gear that may not be used for extended periods requires a strategic approach to long-term storage. This involves not only selecting the right storage environment but also understanding the specific preservation needs of different types of gear. For items such as firearms, electronic devices, and medical supplies, each category demands a unique set of considerations to maintain their functionality over time.

For firearms, controlling humidity is paramount to prevent rust and corrosion. Using dehumidifiers in storage areas or silica gel packs within gun safes can significantly reduce moisture levels. It's essential to clean and oil firearms thoroughly before storage, as this provides a protective barrier against moisture. Additionally, consider using vapor corrosion inhibitors (VCI) within storage containers, which release a corrosion-inhibiting vapor that forms a protective layer on metal surfaces.

Electronic devices, including communication tools and navigation aids, are susceptible to damage from moisture, temperature fluctuations, and electromagnetic pulses (EMPs). To protect these devices, store them in EMP-resistant containers, which can be as simple as a metal garbage can with a tightly sealing lid, lined with a non-conductive material like cardboard. For moisture control, include silica gel packets in each container, and ensure batteries are removed to prevent leakage and corrosion. Store these devices in a cool, dry place, avoiding areas like attics or basements where temperature and humidity levels can fluctuate significantly.

Medical supplies, particularly those with expiration dates like medications and sterile items, require careful monitoring and rotation. Store these supplies in airtight containers to protect against moisture and pests, and keep them in a consistent, cool environment to prevent degradation. Regularly check expiration dates and replace items as needed to ensure your medical kit remains fully functional. For items sensitive to light, such as certain medications and solutions, opaque storage solutions can prevent degradation caused by UV exposure.

In addition to these specific considerations, general principles apply across all types of survival gear. First, ensure all items are cleaned and inspected before being placed into storage. This initial step can prevent the deterioration of materials and identify any maintenance needs before they become problematic. Next, clearly label all containers with contents and the date of storage. This practice not only aids in organization but also in the rotation and inspection process, ensuring that items are easily accessible and in usable condition when needed.

Implementing a regular inspection schedule is crucial for long-term storage. This involves physically checking each item for signs of wear, damage, or expiration. Such inspections can identify issues like seal degradation in airtight containers, battery corrosion in electronic devices, or rust formation on metal surfaces. Addressing these issues promptly ensures that your survival gear remains ready for use at a moment's notice.

Lastly, consider the physical arrangement of stored items, prioritizing accessibility for items that may be needed more urgently. While it's important to utilize space efficiently, ensuring that you can quickly retrieve items like medical supplies or communication devices without having to unpack numerous containers can be critical in an emergency situation.

By adopting these detailed strategies for the long-term storage of survival gear, you can ensure that your equipment remains in optimal condition, ready to serve its purpose when the need arises. This proactive approach to gear maintenance and storage not only protects your investment but also enhances your preparedness level, providing peace of mind that you are well-equipped to handle any situation that may arise.

Assembling Emergency Kits

Assembling emergency kits requires a methodical approach to ensure you are prepared for any situation, whether it be a natural disaster, a home invasion, or an extended power outage. The key is to create kits that are tailored to specific scenarios, ensuring that each kit contains items that are directly relevant to the challenges you might face. This process begins with identifying the types of emergencies most likely to occur in your area, such as hurricanes, wildfires, or earthquakes, and then constructing each kit with those particular circumstances in mind.

For a **basic go-bag**, which is essential for quick evacuations, start with a durable, lightweight backpack that can be easily carried for long distances if necessary. This bag should include non-perishable food items high in calories and nutrition, such as energy bars and ready-to-eat meals that require minimal preparation. Water is critical; include at least one liter per person per day for at least three days. For water purification, pack **portable filters** or **purification tablets** that can treat water from natural sources. Include a **multi-tool** with a knife, pliers, and other essentials, a **hand-crank or battery-powered flashlight**, and a **solar-powered charger** for electronic devices. Personal hygiene items, a first aid kit with personalized medications, and copies of important documents in waterproof containers are also crucial.

For **home survival kits**, which are designed for sheltering in place, consider using large, durable plastic bins that can be sealed to keep out moisture and pests. These should include a more extensive supply of food and water, aiming for a two-week supply per person. Incorporate a variety of canned and dry goods, focusing on nutritional diversity and dietary needs. A comprehensive **first aid kit** should be supplemented with a more extensive range of medical supplies, such as prescription medications, over-the-counter pain relievers, and antibiotics. Include **hygiene supplies** like soap, toothpaste, and toilet paper in larger quantities. For power, consider solar chargers, extra batteries, and a **hand-crank radio** for receiving emergency broadcasts. Tools and supplies for home repair, such as duct tape, plastic sheeting, and basic hand tools, can help manage minor damages to your residence.

Specialized kits may be necessary depending on your location and personal circumstances. For instance, if you live in a cold climate, your car emergency kit should include thermal blankets, a **stove-in-a-can** for heating, and snowshoes if you're in an area where heavy snowfall is common. Conversely, in hot climates, prioritize sun protection, extra water storage solutions, and electrolyte packets to prevent dehydration.

When assembling these kits, always consider the needs of all family members, including pets. **Pet-specific supplies** such as food, water, and a portable carrier should not be overlooked. For children, include comfort items and age-appropriate activities to keep them calm and occupied.

Label each kit clearly and store them in easily accessible locations known to all family members. Regularly review and update the contents of your kits, checking expiration dates on food, water, batteries, and medications. Practicing with your family on how to quickly locate and utilize these kits in an emergency can significantly enhance your collective preparedness and response capability.

Remember, the goal of these emergency kits is not just to survive but to do so with a degree of comfort and security, maintaining your family's health and well-being until the situation stabilizes or help arrives. By meticulously assembling and maintaining your emergency kits, you ensure that you are ready to face a wide range of scenarios with confidence, keeping your loved ones safe and secure in unpredictable times.

Video BONUS

Chapter 10: Tactical Self-Defense Strategies

Basic Self-Defense Techniques

Awareness and Situational Preparedness

In the realm of tactical self-defense and home defense strategies, the cornerstone of ensuring safety begins with cultivating a heightened state of awareness and situational preparedness. This proactive stance involves more than just being vigilant; it's about developing an acute sense of your environment to preemptively identify and mitigate potential threats before they escalate into dire situations. The military often emphasizes the concept of 'situational awareness' as a critical survival skill, which civilians can adapt to enhance their personal and home security. This skill set encompasses observing the nuances of your surroundings, understanding the significance of changes, and making informed decisions quickly.

To build this level of awareness, start by regularly practicing observation skills in your daily life. Pay attention to the normal baseline of your neighborhood's activity patterns, noting the typical ebb and flow of people and vehicles. This familiarity will enable you to detect anomalies or suspicious behaviors more readily. For instance, a car that repeatedly circles the block or unfamiliar individuals loitering without clear purpose might warrant closer attention and possibly, further action such as documenting or reporting to local authorities.

Enhancing situational preparedness also involves understanding the layout and potential vulnerabilities of your home. Regularly assess entry points, ensuring all locks are functional and consider the installation of security systems or cameras as deterrents. Lighting plays a crucial role in home security; ensure that all outdoor areas are well-lit to eliminate shadows where threats could conceal themselves. Motion-sensor lights are particularly effective as they can startle and deter potential intruders while also alerting you to unexpected activity.

Incorporate the practice of 'what-if' scenarios into your routine to mentally and physically prepare for potential situations. For example, consider how you would react if you found your front door ajar upon returning home or if you heard glass breaking in the middle of the night. Planning your response, including how to safely exit your home or where to securely shelter in place, can significantly reduce reaction time during an actual emergency.

Training in basic self-defense techniques is another aspect of situational preparedness. While the hope is never to engage in physical confrontation, having the knowledge and skills to defend oneself can be empowering and may prove critical in a life-threatening situation. This training should also include the use of everyday objects as improvised weapons, from pens and keys to kitchen utensils, understanding their potential to aid in self-defense without the need for specialized weaponry.

Finally, fostering a network of community vigilance can amplify your situational awareness. Engage with neighbors to share observations and establish a collective effort to monitor and report suspicious activities. Many communities benefit from social media groups or neighborhood watch programs that facilitate this type of information sharing, creating a broader safety net for all residents.

By integrating these practices into your daily life, you not only enhance your personal safety and the security of your home but also contribute to the well-being of your community. Situational awareness and preparedness are dynamic skills that evolve with continuous application and adaptation, reflecting the changing nature of the environments in which we live.

Physical Defense Techniques

In the realm of personal safety and home defense, mastering physical defense techniques is indispensable, especially when the situation demands close-quarters engagement. The foundation of effective self-defense lies in understanding and applying basic hand-to-hand combat techniques. These skills are not only crucial for neutralizing threats but also for instilling confidence in one's ability to protect oneself and loved ones in dire situations.

Starting with stance and awareness, the key is to maintain a posture that allows for both stability and mobility. Feet should be shoulder-width apart, knees slightly bent, and body weight distributed evenly on both feet. This position, often referred to as the "fighter's stance," serves as the base for defensive and offensive movements. Awareness of one's surroundings is equally critical, enabling the defender to anticipate and react swiftly to an aggressor's movements.

When it comes to strikes, precision and efficiency outweigh brute strength. Targeting vulnerable points on the attacker's body, such as the eyes, nose, throat, and groin, can incapacitate them long enough to escape or seek help. Techniques such as palm strikes, elbow strikes, and knee strikes are effective and can be executed by individuals of varying strength levels. For instance, a palm strike to the nose or chin can disrupt an attacker's advance, while a well-placed knee to the groin can debilitate them momentarily.

Blocking and evading are fundamental defensive maneuvers that minimize harm and create opportunities for counterattacks. Basic blocks can deflect incoming strikes to vital areas, and evasive movements such as sidestepping or ducking can prevent an attacker from landing a blow. These techniques require practice to develop reflexive responses that can be deployed under stress.

In situations where physical confrontation is unavoidable, everyday objects can be transformed into improvised weapons to enhance one's defensive capabilities. Items such as pens, keys, flashlights, and even hot beverages can be used to deter or disable an attacker. For example, a pen, held securely, can be used to deliver targeted strikes to sensitive areas, while keys, clutched in a fist with the key points protruding between the fingers, can serve as a makeshift knuckle duster.

Training and preparedness are paramount for effectively employing physical defense techniques and improvised weapons. Regular practice under various scenarios increases muscle memory, reaction time, and decision-making under pressure, ensuring that one is better prepared to face potential threats. Additionally, engaging in self-defense classes or workshops conducted by experienced instructors can provide valuable hands-on experience and feedback, further honing one's skills.

It is important to remember that the primary goal of self-defense is personal safety. Avoiding confrontation through situational awareness and de-escalation techniques should always be the first line of defense. However, when faced with an imminent threat, having a repertoire of physical defense techniques and the knowledge of how to use everyday objects as improvised weapons can make a significant difference in the outcome of a dangerous encounter.

De-escalation and Conflict Resolution

De-escalation and conflict resolution are critical components of self-defense that prioritize safety and aim to prevent situations from escalating into violence. The essence of de-escalation lies in using verbal communication and body language to diffuse potentially dangerous situations, thereby protecting oneself and others without resorting to physical confrontation. This approach aligns with the principle of using the minimum force necessary to ensure safety, emphasizing the strategic aspect of self-defense that extends beyond physical capabilities to include psychological and communication skills.

The first step in effective de-escalation is to maintain a calm and composed demeanor. This involves controlling one's tone of voice to keep it even and non-threatening, as well as adopting a relaxed body posture that signals non-aggression. Making deliberate choices about one's words and actions can significantly influence the outcome of a tense situation. For instance, using open-ended questions to engage the other person can shift the dynamic from confrontation to conversation, providing an opportunity to find common ground or a peaceful resolution.

Another vital aspect of de-escalation is active listening. By showing genuine interest in the other person's concerns and viewpoints, one can often identify the root cause of the conflict and work towards addressing it. Active listening involves making eye contact, nodding to acknowledge the other's points, and summarizing their statements to demonstrate understanding. This technique can help de-escalate emotions and pave the way for rational discussion.

Maintaining situational awareness is also crucial during conflict resolution. This means being mindful of one's environment, including potential escape routes, the presence of bystanders who could offer assistance, and any objects that could be used as weapons by an aggressor. By staying aware of these factors, one can better navigate the situation and make informed decisions about when to engage in dialogue, when to create distance, and when to seek help.

In some cases, offering a concession or compromise can be an effective strategy for de-escalating a conflict. This does not mean surrendering or compromising one's safety but rather finding a temporary solution that can diffuse tension and prevent violence. For example, agreeing to move a discussion to a neutral location or postponing it to a later time when both parties are calmer can provide an immediate reduction in hostility.

It's important to recognize the signs that de-escalation efforts are not working and to be prepared to change tactics. If the other person becomes increasingly agitated, refuses to engage in dialogue, or exhibits signs of imminent violence, prioritizing physical safety becomes paramount. This may involve creating distance, finding a barrier, or preparing to defend oneself if necessary.

Throughout any attempt at de-escalation, the goal remains to protect oneself and others while minimizing harm. By employing strategic communication and conflict resolution techniques, individuals can navigate tense situations more effectively, reducing the likelihood of violence and ensuring a safer outcome for all involved.

Tactical Tools and Weapons

Tactical Weapons for Home Defense

Selecting the right tactical weapons for home defense requires a nuanced understanding of both the potential threats and the specific environment of your home. The cornerstone of this selection process is identifying the types of weapons that will provide you and your family with the highest level of security while also considering legal, ethical, and practical aspects.

Firearms are often the first category that comes to mind when discussing home defense. The choice of a firearm, whether it's a handgun, shotgun, or rifle, should be guided by several factors including ease of use, reliability, and the user's proficiency. Handguns, for example, are compact and easier to maneuver within the confined spaces of a home. They can be quickly accessed in an emergency. However, their effective use requires regular training to maintain proficiency. Shotguns, with their wider spread, offer a margin of error in high-stress situations, making them suitable for individuals with varying levels of shooting experience. Rifles, while offering greater accuracy and range, may not be the best choice for all home environments due to their size and the potential for over-penetration.

Knives and other bladed weapons serve as both practical tools and defensive weapons. In close-quarters defense, a sturdy, fixed-blade knife can be invaluable. The choice of a knife should consider the blade length, which ideally should not exceed six inches for ease of handling, and the grip, which must be secure even in wet conditions. Training in basic knife defense techniques is also essential to effectively wield a knife in a defensive scenario.

Non-lethal weapons provide an alternative for those uncomfortable with the idea of lethal force or in situations where lethal force is not warranted. Pepper spray, for example, can incapacitate an attacker, allowing you to escape or call for help. It's effective at a range, which provides a safety buffer between you and the threat. Stun guns and tasers are other options, delivering an electric shock to temporarily disable an assailant. The choice of a non-lethal weapon should be accompanied by an understanding of its effective range, the legal regulations governing its use, and proper training to ensure it can be deployed effectively under stress.

When selecting tactical weapons for home defense, consider the layout of your home and the likely scenarios in which you would need to use these weapons. A multi-story home may require different considerations than a single-floor apartment. The presence of children or other dependents also influences the choice of weapons and their storage solutions to prevent accidents.

In addition to selecting the appropriate weapons, developing a comprehensive home defense plan is crucial. This plan should include safe rooms, escape routes, and communication strategies with family members and local law enforcement. Regular training and drills that involve all household members will ensure that everyone knows how to respond in an emergency.

Ultimately, the effectiveness of any tactical weapon for home defense lies not just in the weapon itself but in the hands of the trained, responsible individual wielding it. Regular training, legal awareness, and a clear understanding of your own ethical boundaries regarding the use of force are all critical components of responsible weapon ownership for home defense.

Tactical Tools Training and Proficiency

Regular training with your selected tactical tools is not just a recommendation; it's a necessity for ensuring the safety and security of your home and loved ones. The effectiveness of any weapon, whether it's a firearm, knife, or non-lethal device, is significantly enhanced by the user's proficiency and confidence in handling it. This section delves into the critical aspects of training and developing proficiency with your tactical tools, focusing on methods to improve accuracy, speed, and decision-making in high-pressure situations.

To begin, establishing a consistent training schedule is paramount. This routine should include dedicated time for both dry fire exercises and live fire practice at a range, if firearms are part of your tactical toolkit. Dry fire practice, which involves handling the weapon and practicing trigger pulls without live ammunition, is invaluable for improving muscle memory and ensuring smooth, efficient weapon manipulation. It allows you to focus on stance, grip, sight alignment, and trigger control without the distraction of recoil and noise. For safety, always ensure your firearm is unloaded during dry fire practice and maintain a safe direction.

For those incorporating knives or other bladed weapons into their home defense strategy, training involves familiarizing oneself with the weapon's balance, optimal grip, and effective striking techniques. Practice drawing the knife from its sheath or your pocket, as quick access is crucial in an emergency. Utilize training blades to safely practice defensive maneuvers and attacks against targets or during controlled sparring sessions with a partner.

Incorporating non-lethal options like pepper spray or stun guns also requires practice. Familiarize yourself with the deployment mechanism, range, and effects of these tools. Practice drawing and aiming your non-lethal device, just as you would with a more lethal option. Understanding the operational nuances of these devices, including safety switches and effective ranges, can make a significant difference in a high-stress encounter.

Speed and accuracy under pressure are honed through scenario-based training, which simulates real-life situations you might encounter. This type of training helps develop quick decision-making skills, teaching you to rapidly assess threats and respond appropriately. Incorporate stress inoculation techniques into your training by introducing physical exertion before weapon drills, simulating the elevated heart rate and adrenaline rush experienced during an actual defense scenario.

Regularly attending professionally led training courses offers structured learning and feedback from experienced instructors. These courses can introduce you to advanced tactics, provide opportunities to train under stress, and expose you to a variety of scenarios that challenge your decision-making skills. Additionally, engaging with a community of like-minded individuals fosters a supportive environment for sharing knowledge and experiences, further enhancing your skill set.

Finally, maintaining your tactical tools is as crucial as training with them. Regular cleaning, inspection, and necessary maintenance ensure your weapons function reliably when needed. Familiarize yourself with the disassembly and reassembly of your firearms, understand the care needed for your knives to keep them sharp and rust-free, and regularly check the battery life and functionality of non-lethal devices.

By dedicating time to regular, comprehensive training, you not only improve your technical skills with your chosen tactical tools but also enhance your mental preparedness for the unexpected. This commitment to preparedness transforms your tactical tools from mere objects into extensions of your own capabilities, ensuring you are always ready to defend your home and loved ones effectively.

Legal Aspects of Home Defense Weapons

Understanding the legal framework surrounding the use of weapons for home defense is paramount to ensure that your protective measures do not inadvertently place you on the wrong side of the law. The right to defend oneself and one's family is deeply ingrained in American culture and legal systems, yet it is bounded by specific conditions and regulations that vary significantly from state to state. When considering the integration of firearms or any tactical tools into your home defense strategy, a comprehensive grasp of local, state, and federal laws is essential. This includes not only the legal acquisition and possession of firearms but also the circumstances under which their use is justified.

The cornerstone of legal self-defense in the home is the doctrine known as "Castle Doctrine," a principle adopted by many states that allows individuals to use reasonable force, including deadly force, to protect themselves against an intruder within their home. This doctrine is predicated on the notion that one's home is a sanctuary where the homeowner has the right to protect themselves without the duty to retreat. However, the interpretation of what constitutes reasonable force and the specifics of when and how force can be lawfully used vary. Some states extend this protection to include not just the physical dwelling but also attached areas such as porches and garages, while others may require that the intruder be committing a forcible felony.

In states with "Stand Your Ground" laws, the principle of no duty to retreat is extended beyond the home to any place a person has a legal right to be. These laws allow individuals to use force in self-defense when there is a reasonable belief of a threat, without the obligation to attempt to escape the situation. It is critical to understand whether your state adheres to the Castle Doctrine, Stand Your Ground laws, or a combination of both, and the specific requirements and limitations of these laws.

The legal considerations for the use of weapons in home defense also encompass the manner of weapon storage and accessibility. Many jurisdictions have specific regulations designed to prevent accidents and unauthorized access, especially by children. Safe storage laws may dictate the use of gun safes, trigger locks, or other security measures. Non-compliance with these regulations can lead to legal repercussions in the event of an accidental discharge or if a firearm is accessed by a minor.

Another pivotal aspect is the distinction between lethal and non-lethal force. While firearms are the most definitive form of lethal force, non-lethal weapons such as stun guns, pepper spray, and tasers are regulated differently. Some states require permits for carrying these devices, and their use is subject to legal scrutiny regarding the proportionality of the response to the perceived threat.

Before incorporating any form of weapon into your home defense plan, it is advisable to consult with a legal professional specializing in self-defense and firearms law in your jurisdiction. This can provide clarity on the lawful purchase, registration, and use of tactical tools for home defense. Additionally, staying informed about changes in legislation and participating in firearms safety and legal responsibility training courses can further safeguard against legal complications.

Engaging with local law enforcement or attending community meetings on public safety can also offer insights into the legal landscape and community standards regarding home defense. These interactions not only foster a better understanding of your rights and responsibilities but also contribute to a cooperative relationship with local authorities, which can be invaluable in times of crisis.

In essence, the legal considerations for using weapons in home defense underscore the importance of informed, responsible ownership and usage. By ensuring compliance with all applicable laws and regulations, you protect not only your home and loved ones but also your legal standing, ensuring that your defensive actions are within the bounds of the law.

Defensive Tactics Against Intruders

Establishing a Defensive Perimeter

Establishing a defensive perimeter around your home is a critical first step in ensuring the safety and security of your loved ones. This process involves a meticulous assessment of your property to identify potential vulnerabilities and implement measures to fortify these areas against intruders. Begin by conducting a thorough walk-around of your property during both day and night to understand how visibility, access points, and natural or man-made barriers can be optimized for defense. Pay special attention to areas that are obscured by shadows or dense foliage, as these can provide cover for potential intruders.

The use of **lighting** plays a pivotal role in deterring unauthorized entry. Install motion-activated floodlights around the perimeter of your property, focusing on entry points and dark areas to eliminate hiding spots. Opt for LED bulbs for their longevity and energy efficiency, ensuring that the lumens rating (brightness) is high enough to illuminate the intended area effectively. Position lights at a height that cannot be easily tampered with and angle them in a way that maximizes coverage without causing light pollution to neighboring properties.

Barriers such as fences and walls are physical impediments that can significantly enhance your home's security. A well-constructed fence should be at least 8 feet tall to deter climbing, with posts buried deep enough to prevent undermining. Materials like metal or solid wood offer robust resistance against forced entry, but ensure there are no horizontal elements that could aid an intruder in climbing. Incorporating prickly or thorny plants along the fence line can add an additional layer of natural defense. For gates, select designs that are both sturdy and lockable, preferably with a mechanism that is not easily picked or broken.

Surveillance systems are your eyes when you cannot physically monitor your property. High-definition cameras should be placed at all entry points, with coverage extending to the driveway, garage, and any outbuildings. Opt for models with night vision capabilities to ensure round-the-clock monitoring. Consider the integration of cameras into a smart home security system that can send real-time alerts to your mobile device upon detecting motion. This allows for immediate action, whether it's verifying a false alarm or contacting law enforcement in the event of an intrusion attempt.

In addition to these measures, **clear signage** indicating the presence of a security system can act as a psychological barrier, often deterring would-be intruders from attempting entry. However, avoid specifying the brand of your security system, as this can provide determined intruders with valuable information on how to bypass it.

Remember, the goal of establishing a defensive perimeter is not just to prevent unauthorized entry but to create layers of defense that make it increasingly difficult for an intruder to access your home without detection. This involves a combination of physical barriers, surveillance technology, and strategic lighting to cover all potential points of entry. By implementing these measures, you transform your home into a fortress that prioritizes the safety and security of its inhabitants, ensuring peace of mind in an uncertain world.

Safe Room Tactics and Protocols

Designing and utilizing a safe room effectively during a home invasion requires meticulous planning and understanding of best practices to ensure the safety and security of your loved ones. The primary function of a safe room is to act as a fortified sanctuary in the event of an intrusion, providing a secure space where family members can retreat until help arrives or the threat is neutralized. To achieve this, several critical factors must be considered, from the safe room's location and construction to the supplies it contains and the communication tools available within.

Firstly, the location of your safe room is paramount. Ideally, it should be situated in a part of the house that is easily accessible to all family members but not obvious to intruders. Common choices include a reinforced closet, a basement area, or even a specially designed space within a master bedroom. The key is to ensure that the location does not trap you or provide easy access for an intruder to compromise the safe room. It should have no windows to the outside and only one solid core door with reinforced hinges and a deadbolt lock for entry, making it harder for intruders to gain access.

The construction of the safe room should utilize materials that are resistant to forced entry. Walls can be reinforced with steel panels or Kevlar lining, offering bullet-resistant protection. The door should be made of steel or solid wood with a deadbolt lock, and if possible, the room should be equipped with a ventilation system that can be securely closed to prevent any external access. Additionally, the inclusion of a peephole or a small, reinforced window in the door allows you to see outside without opening it.

Inside the safe room, you should stock essential supplies that will support you for at least 72 hours. This includes bottled water, non-perishable food items, first aid supplies, flashlights with extra batteries, a portable toilet, and blankets. Communication tools are crucial; therefore, a charged cell phone with an external battery pack, a landline connection, or a two-way radio should be available to contact emergency services. It's also wise to include a list of important contacts and a copy of your family emergency plan.

Developing a family emergency plan is a critical step in ensuring everyone knows what to do in the event of an intrusion. This plan should include clear instructions on how to reach the safe room from different parts of the house, a code word to signal when to retreat to the safe room, and roles for each family member, such as who is responsible for grabbing the emergency kit or who should call 911. Regular drills should be conducted to ensure everyone is familiar with the plan and can execute it under stress.

Evacuation routes from the safe room should also be planned in case the intruder attempts to compromise the safe room or in the event of a fire. This could involve a hidden exit that leads outside or a method to safely exit the room once law enforcement has secured the property. Communication with emergency responders is critical; they should be informed that a safe room is being utilized and provided with its location within the house to expedite rescue efforts.

In conclusion, the effective use of a safe room during a home invasion hinges on thorough preparation and clear communication. By selecting an optimal location, reinforcing its structure, stocking it with essential supplies, and integrating it into a comprehensive family emergency plan, you can significantly enhance your household's security and resilience in the face of intrusions. Regular review and practice of these protocols ensure that, in a moment of crisis, your family can respond swiftly and decisively to protect themselves.

Responding to a Home Invasion

Materials

- High-quality deadbolt locks for all exterior doors
- Window locks and security film for glass reinforcement
- Exterior-grade, motion-activated lighting for the perimeter of the property
- Security cameras with night vision and remote monitoring capabilities
- Solid core or metal exterior doors
- A loud, easily accessible alarm system
- Communication devices (cell phone, landline with battery backup, two-way radios)
- Self-defense tools (pepper spray, stun gun) accessible in multiple rooms
- Safe room supplies (water, non-perishable food, first aid kit, flashlights, extra batteries)

Tools

- Drill and drill bits for installing locks and lighting
- Screwdrivers for lock installation and adjustments
- Hammer and nails for securing windows with plywood (if necessary)
- Ladder for installing motion-activated lighting and security cameras
- Smartphone or computer for monitoring security cameras and contacting authorities

Safety measures

- Ensure all tools are used according to manufacturer instructions to prevent injury.
- When installing security equipment, follow all safety guidelines to avoid electrical hazards.
- Keep self-defense tools out of reach of children and in known, easily accessible locations for adults.

Step-by-step instructions

1. **Secure Entry Points:** Install high-quality deadbolt locks on all exterior doors. Reinforce door frames and hinges to resist forced entry. Apply security film to windows to make them harder to break, and install locks on all windows.

2. **Illuminate the Exterior:** Set up exterior-grade, motion-activated lighting around the perimeter of your home to deter intruders by eliminating dark spots.

3. **Install Surveillance:** Place security cameras at all entry points and common areas, ensuring they have night vision and remote monitoring capabilities for real-time surveillance.

4. **Alarm System Setup:** Install a loud alarm system that can be easily activated. Consider systems that automatically alert local authorities when triggered.

5. **Prepare Communication Devices:** Ensure you have multiple ways to communicate with the outside world. Keep a charged cell phone, a landline with battery backup, and two-way radios in case of power failure.

6. **Access to Self-defense Tools:** Place pepper spray, stun guns, or other non-lethal self-defense tools in strategic, easily accessible locations throughout your home.

7. **Safe Room Preparation:** Designate a safe room with solid core or metal doors. Stock it with essential supplies like water, non-perishable food, a first aid kit, flashlights, and extra batteries.

8. **Practice Emergency Protocols:** Regularly review and practice your home invasion response plan with all household members. Include how to use the alarm system, where to find self-defense tools, and how to access the safe room.

9. **Stay Informed:** Keep a smartphone or computer handy to monitor security cameras and call for help if an intruder is detected. Teach all capable household members how to use these devices to contact authorities.

10. **Responding to an Intrusion:** If an intruder enters your home, prioritize getting to your safe room and calling for help. Use self-defense tools only as a last resort and focus on staying safe until authorities arrive.

Safety tips

- Regularly check the batteries in your security cameras, alarm system, and flashlights.
- Test and maintain your home security system to ensure it's functioning correctly.
- Educate all household members on the importance of not opening doors to strangers and how to activate the home alarm system.

Maintenance

- Monthly: Test alarm systems and check security camera batteries and functionality.
- Quarterly: Inspect locks, window reinforcements, and exterior lighting for any signs of wear or damage.
- Annually: Review and update your home invasion response plan based on any changes in household or security technology advancements.

Difficulty rating ★★★☆☆

Variations

- For homes without the option for a dedicated safe room, identify a lockable room with a phone line or good cell service as an emergency hideout.
- In areas with higher crime rates, consider adding a monitored security service for an extra layer of protection and peace of mind.

Video BONUS

Conclusion

Key Concepts and Strategies Recap

Throughout this guide, we've delved into the critical aspects of transforming your home into a secure survival fortress, drawing inspiration from military principles to enhance your preparedness and resilience. We began by understanding the concept of bugging in, emphasizing the strategic advantage of fortifying your existing stronghold rather than evacuating. The psychological shift required for this commitment was explored, preparing you for the isolation and challenges of long-term survival in a secure environment.

We assessed the importance of evaluating your geographical location and environmental factors, which play a pivotal role in deciding whether to bug in. This decision-making process was supported by a comprehensive home assessment guide, pinpointing vulnerabilities and strengths in your home's current security setup. A step-by-step plan was outlined to create a customized bug-in strategy, involving all household members to ensure a unified approach.

The guide stressed the significance of avoiding common pitfalls such as overconfidence and complacency, urging continuous vigilance and preparation. Developing a military mindset was identified as crucial, with emphasis on discipline, mental toughness, and the adaptation of military principles for civilian preparedness.

Physical resilience was addressed through fitness routines tailored to survival scenarios, alongside strategies for managing stress and maintaining morale during prolonged emergencies. The book provided detailed instructions on home security enhancements, from conducting a security audit to fortifying entry points and implementing surveillance systems.

Safe room design and construction were covered extensively, ensuring you have a secure retreat within your home. Long-term food storage and water security were discussed in depth, offering strategies for stockpiling, rotation, and ensuring the nutritional needs of your household are met.

Off-grid energy solutions, medical preparedness, crisis communication, and essential survival gear were explored, equipping you with the knowledge to maintain independence and safety in various crisis scenarios. Finally, tactical self-defense and home defense strategies were presented, empowering you with the skills and confidence to protect your loved ones effectively.

By embracing these concepts and strategies, you are now better prepared to face emergencies with a comprehensive plan, ensuring the safety and security of your household.

Final Thoughts on Preparedness and Resilience

As we wrap up our exploration into the world of military-inspired home fortification and survival strategies, it's essential to recognize that preparedness and resilience are not just about the physical measures we put in place. They are about a mindset, a way of life that prioritizes the safety and security of our loved ones. The journey towards becoming a survivor and strategist in your own right involves continuous learning, adaptation, and vigilance. The principles and techniques detailed throughout this guide serve as a foundation, a starting point from which you can expand and tailor your approach to meet the specific needs of your household and circumstances. Remember, the goal is not to live in fear but to empower yourself and your family with the knowledge and skills to face whatever challenges may come with confidence. The true strength of a fortress lies not just in its walls but in the resolve and preparedness of those who dwell within. As you move forward, keep in mind the importance of regular drills, updates to your plans and supplies, and staying informed about the latest in home security and survival tactics. Engage with your community, share knowledge, and build a network of support, for in unity there is strength. The path to preparedness is ongoing, a perpetual commitment to ensuring the well-being of those you hold dear. Let the strategies outlined here be your guide, but always be ready to adapt, innovate, and overcome.

Next Steps in Preparedness

Building on your preparedness skills is an ongoing process that requires dedication, continuous learning, and practical application. As you move forward, focus on expanding your knowledge base by exploring advanced topics in survival strategies, home fortification techniques, and self-defense mechanisms. Engage with communities, both online and in-person, that share a passion for emergency preparedness and home security. These platforms can offer invaluable insights, real-world experiences, and innovative solutions to common and uncommon challenges. Participate in workshops and training sessions that provide hands-on experience with survival skills, medical first aid, and tactical defense. These opportunities not only enhance your capabilities but also allow you to network with experts and like-minded individuals who can offer support and guidance.

Regularly review and update your bug-in plan and emergency kits to reflect any changes in your living situation, advancements in technology, or shifts in the threat landscape. This includes reassessing your food and water storage strategies, ensuring your medical supplies are within their expiration dates, and verifying that all electronic devices and communication tools are in working order and compatible with current technologies. Experiment with renewable energy sources, such as solar panels or wind turbines, to understand their potential benefits and limitations for your specific geographical location and energy needs. This hands-on approach will give you a deeper understanding of how to maintain and optimize these systems for long-term sustainability.

Stay informed about the latest developments in home security systems, including smart home technologies that offer enhanced monitoring and control over your property's safety. Evaluate these options critically, considering their integration with your existing security measures and their effectiveness in your particular environment.

Lastly, prioritize physical fitness and mental resilience. The ability to respond effectively to emergencies is as much about physical preparedness as it is about having the right tools and knowledge. Incorporate regular exercise, stress management techniques, and scenario-based training into your routine to ensure you are physically and mentally equipped to handle whatever challenges may arise.

Made in United States
Troutdale, OR
02/13/2025